Date Smart!

Date Smart!

How to Stop Revolving and Start Evolving in Your Relationships

DAVID D. COLEMAN AND
M. RICHARD DOYLE

PRIMA PUBLISHING

Published by Prima Publishing, Roseville, California. Member of the Crown Publishing Group, a division of Random House, Inc., New York.

PRIMA PUBLISHING and colophon are trademarks of Random House, Inc., registered with the United States Patent and Trademark Office.

Products mentioned are trademarks of their respective companies.

Library of Congress Cataloging-in-Publication Data

Coleman, David D.
    Date smart : how to stop revolving and start evolving in relationships / David D. Coleman and M. Richard Doyle.
        p.   cm.
    Includes index.
    ISBN 0-7615-2173-9
    1. Dating (Social customs)—United States. 2. Man-woman relationships—United States. I. Doyle, M. Richard. II. Title.

HQ801 .C665 1999
646.7'7—dc21

                                                                99-048743

03 04 05 DD 10 9 8 7 6 5 4 3
Printed in the United States of America

First Edition

Visit us online at www.primapublishing.com

DEDICATIONS

By David: To my father, Marvin, who was my best friend and biggest fan for 37 years and to my mother, Vivian, who has taught me the meaning of unconditional love and courage. Also, to my wife, Diane, and daughters Shannon and Natalie who allowed their husband and father all the time necessary to write a book that took him away from them.

By Rick: To my sister, Marty Sena, for her love and support. My mother, Ann, and father, Dick, whom I miss more than I can describe. Thank you for believing in me, always.

I am becoming the person you always intended me to be.

CONTENTS

ACKNOWLEDGMENTS

We are grateful to acknowledge the assistance, support, encouragement and contributions of the following people who have positively impacted our lives and helped to make this book possible:

Gail Coleman
Michelle Rathman
Gregg DeCrane
 & Family
Sara Pearce
Karen, Bob,
 Allyson &
 Michael Cheslock
Andrea Pedolsky
Dave Goodman
Ellen Lytle
Jo Hacha
Tom DeLuca
Jim Comodeca
Sara Schlossman
MaryBeth Fontana
Edward "Chip" Cole, Jr.
Christine Ivanov
Crystal Bertrand
Sally Watson
Prima Publishing
Carol Miller
Dale and Eleanor
 Grinstead
Stewart Susskind
Alex and Carol Aronis
Donna and Larry
 Spengler
Monica Clark &
 Family
Tom Misuraca

Reyne and Dan Kaiser
Rob Calvert
Anne Bakker Gras
Boyd Jones
Dan, Kim, Brittany
 & Breanne Grinstead
Tony Bender
Karen DiAsio
Jim Knippenberg
Dave Roberts
Dan Guy
Don Wegman
Mona Morrow
Kevin and Deanne
 Leland
Terri and Lora Trost
Mary Catherine Dean
Melissa Keller
Dave Reynolds
Brenda Merrick
Ron Lloyd
Glenn Farr & NACA
Rick Morgan
W. C. Kirby
Loni and Sue
 Sykos, Hana
 Fantasy Flowers
Harley Davidson
Matt Jarrett
Marilyn Moaro
Libby Larson

Johnna and Rick
 Grinstead
David Hansen
Liz and Marshall
 Reaney
Doug and Renee
 Wong
Kim Robinson
Michelle Robson
Sheila Fidelman &
 Family
Don and Kate Bricker
Gretchen Laatsch
Daylle Schwartz
Tanya Reed
Malcolm and Joy Reed
Dr. John Jameson
Mike Swank
Sandy, Stan & Tim
 Martin
Tracey Bender

and all of our
audience members,
previous clients,
media fans, and
column followers.

INTRODUCTION

Why did we write this book? We knew from experience that a large number of people were either involved in unhappy, unhealthy, and unsuccessful relationships, or had given up on being involved in a positive one at all. We felt strongly that a comprehensive, yet light-hearted book that addressed the causes and conditions for these failures and offered simple, practical solutions would greatly benefit many of you.

Our goal is to help you become the person you desire to be and to attract and maintain the love that you want and need in your life. The layout of the book is simple. Chapters one through four contain assessments and exercises to help you pinpoint specific aspects of your personality and character that have caused you to pick poorly, remain in unhealthy relationships, or sabotage healthy ones. Not everyone will relate to every exercise. While we strongly encourage you to complete all the assessments and exercises, understand that we're including tools for our general audience and some may not apply directly to you. Be objective and don't pass over all of them if you feel that one particular piece doesn't speak directly to you. The next one probably will. Keep in mind that the solutions will follow and each chapter and exercise builds upon the previous one.

In chapter five, we'll show you that the lack of success in your relationship isn't all your fault. Societal, cultural, and systemic influences play a large part in your relationship failures. Chapter six provides solutions to resolving the core issues you'll identify in chapters one through four and gives you tools to build a healthy relationship with an available person and identify when a person is worth pursuing. It's not just enough to start a relationship. You must understand its evolution, key characteristics, and how to nurture and maintain it for long-term success. This will be covered in chapter seven. Chapters eight and nine focus on developing and maintaining long-term stability and romance as well as exercises to enhance, strengthen, or end a relationship, no matter what condition it's in.

Our primary focus for the book is not to fix you. We intend to ruin your dysfunction by making you alert and aware of the causes and conditions that set you up to fail. When they become obvious, you'll no longer do what you used to and can practice the new, healthy behavior learned in this book. Repeated failure in relationships, whether short or long-term, can be brutally painful in some cases. That's why we kept our sense of humor as we wrote this. While we cover serious subjects, we've found that laughter and coming to a realization that you're not alone can help lift any loneliness you may feel. As you turn the pages, some of you may open up emotional floodgates and be tempted to put the book aside prematurely. If we're bringing up that kind of emotion, it means that we're identifying what needs to be changed. The solutions will be next. Please read this book to its conclusion. If you follow the directions and suggestions without deviation for a period of at least six months, we're sure you'll see a 180 degree turnaround!

If the book is too painful at times to get through on your own, we strongly encourage going through it with a qualified therapist. The book includes our personal insights, our experiences, and exercises we've created. However, we sometimes quote other people and have included information from a variety of proven sources to give you a well-rounded picture of how to achieve relationship success. We believe this book will be a powerful tool for making the changes needed, to give you confidence and courage to make them and will allow you to achieve the type of relationship you deserve and desire.

Our schedules no longer allow us to meet every person individually or answer each question we receive, but we encourage you to sponsor or attend our live seminars (as listed on www.datingdoctor.com) as well as encourage your favorite newspaper or magazine to carry our column. If you follow our suggestions to the best of your ability, *Date Smart!* may be the last self-help book on relationships you'll ever need.

Date Smart!

Are You a Loser Magnet?

On a cold winter day, a woman wearing a warm coat was strolling along a path and heard a hissing noise. "Psssst. Miss? Miss?" She turned around and spotted a poisonous snake. It said, "Miss, I'm freezing. Please put me in your coat so I can get warm."

The woman knew better and replied, "No, you're a poisonous snake. If I do what you ask, you'll bite me and I'll die." She continued down the path.

Moments later the snake became more persistent. "Pssssssst!" She made eye contact and he once again pleaded his case, "Please, Miss, I don't want to freeze to death. Just let me warm up under your coat for awhile. I promise not to hurt you."

The woman repeated with conviction, "No, you're dangerous to me. If I pick you up, I know you'll bite me and I'll die." She continued on her way.

The snake changed tactics, using his sneakier nature to appeal to her emotions by saying, "Please, Miss, I'm one of God's creatures. You're a good person and can't let me freeze to death. Please warm me inside your coat."

This caring woman softened and asked, "Do you promise not to bite me?"

To this the snake replied, "Yes, I promise."

She allowed her emotions to override her judgment and placed the snake inside her coat. She felt him slowly coil around her waist as he settled in. It was reminiscent of the warmth of a first embrace. Suddenly, his razor sharp teeth sank into her flesh. As she realized her mistake, pain, fear, regret, anxiety, and depression set in. As she fell to the ground, fatally wounded, the snake slithered away.

The woman asked, "Why did you bite me? You promised you wouldn't hurt me."

The snake coiled, and stared back at her without remorse. With the callousness of an old pro who had exploited another victim, the snake made her recall what she'd chosen to ignore, "You knew what I was when you picked me up."

Does this snakebite story sound familiar? We often put aside what we've learned from bad experiences when we're once again tempted to believe in someone. How many times have you entered a relationship *knowing* that the person may end up hurting you? We meet someone we're attracted to and are tempted. When someone tempts us, we tend to make excuses that allow us to ignore our better judgment, to close our ears to warnings from people who care about us. We want to believe that "This time will be different." Then later, as we lick our wounds, we wonder, "Why does this always happen to me? From bitten to wounded to scarred—when will it change?" Victims come in male and female versions. So do snakes.

Can you stop this cycle of getting into relationships that aren't good for you? Absolutely! We intend to show you why many of us make bad relationship choices and to help you attract someone who will be a good partner in a satisfying relationship. Even if you've been attracting unhealthy people your whole life, you *can* have a relationship that will

bring you joy, comfort, and support, rather than one that will have you on edge all the time. Sound good? Then keep reading. Happiness in a relationship can be yours once you understand why you keep getting into ones that aren't healthy and learn how to use the tools we'll provide to make healthier choices in the future. You *can* do it!

REVOLVING-DOOR RELATIONSHIPS

Have you seen yourself as the victim of one or more snakebites over the years? The snake's victim, like many of you, has what we refer to as a **Broken Picker**. This means she picked or chose to interact with a dangerous entity with visible warning signs, knowing full well what he was and what unhappy consequences a relationship with him could bring. A snake can easily tempt both sexes; likewise, having a Broken Picker is not gender-specific (our victim could have easily been a man). The danger for many of you has been choosing a person who is emotionally unavailable, or picking someone who is so unhealthy that their character or behavior will surely result in a destructive, unsuccessful relationship.

How many times have you picked the wrong person or stayed in a relationship too long? After ending one, have you immediately gotten involved in another that was just as bad or worse? How many times have you crossed back over a "burned bridge" to a person you swore you'd never see again? Do you use rationalizations you already know don't work, such as: "He promised to change." "She said she'd get help." "I'll never be treated like that again." "This time things will be different." But things never are different.

Have you watched friends and family members go from marriage to marriage, separation to separation, and divorce to divorce, and heard them lament, "Why does this keep happening to me?" "Where is my perfect match?" "Why can't I find someone who's right for me?" "Why doesn't someone find me?" "When am I going to get a break?" They lament but rarely learn. Those who are single, lonely, or stuck in a dead-end relationship can relate all too well.

What we identify as **Revolving-Door Relationships** result from poor picking. They represent how we go in and out and in and out and in and out of unhealthy relationships without understanding why we enter or how we can exit the revolving-door cycle. We continue the pattern because it's what we know. Ending up in a relationship with the wrong person can be easier than choosing a healthy, well-rounded partner.

> 66 Ending up in a relationship with the wrong person can be easier than choosing a healthy, well-rounded partner. 99

With each poor choice we get further from finding someone who's good for us. After a series of unhealthy relationships, would you even recognize a healthy one? First we'll show you the three categories of revolving-door relationships: The Burned Bridge, The Browser, and The Desert. Once you can identify the one(s) you've experienced, we'll give you the tools to fix your Broken Picker so you can attract someone with whom you can experience a healthy and satisfying relationship.

THE BURNED BRIDGE

The Burned Bridge relationship is one in which you return to a bad relationship. Despite the fact that it ended the first time for painful

reasons, you still return, mainly for the wrong reasons—financial security, loneliness, jealousy, sex, children, anger, or to prove everyone else "wrong" by "making it work this time." You repeat the old refrain that keeps us going back for more—"This time will be different." It rarely is. You put yourself through more unhappiness, frustration, and disappointment before accepting that nothing changed.

The burned-bridge relationship ends because only one of you travels back over the burned bridge—you! Since neither of you has changed significantly, the situation can't be much different than it originally was. There was no major effort made or new approach used to change how the relationship functioned in the first place. A 100% failure rate is inevitable. If it walks like a duck, talks like a duck, sounds like a duck— surprise—it's a duck! Open your eyes and ears and hear the familiar quacking before you return to a bad relationship again.

He has slept with your best friend and sister. You never want to see him again. You proclaim that you've "had enough and are never going back again." Three weeks later, you're back. You returned because he needed you and you're the only one in the world for him. It feels like old times, like courtship the first time. He's charming, attentive, a perfect gentleman. Four months later, he's back to making passes at everyone in a skirt.

Why is he unfaithful? Because he knows you'll tolerate it. Your threats to end the relationship for good are groundless. He knows you'll take him back if he says the right words and makes the right promises. He gets away with doing what hurts you, so why should he stop? It can take many more rounds before you're fed up enough to break the cycle, but it doesn't have to. You can burn that bridge down without regret or remorse, and blaze a new trail to happiness. As you build a strong

relationship with a healthy partner, you can traverse even the greatest ravines that in the past would have prompted you to turn back.

THE BROWSER

The so-called **Browser** relationship terminates in three weeks or less for a variety of reasons. It's a bad "date du jour" (date of the day!). Typical dates a browser might experience are:

◇ **Date #1:** Three weeks go by before you decide this person is not your "type." (Hello? It took you three weeks?)

◇ **Date #2:** Three weeks later, you realize you have nothing in common.

◇ **Date #3:** Three weeks later, you've scored, you're bored, and you need a new toy.

◇ **Date #4:** Three weeks later, the flame burns out. (It was too intense, too much, too fast, too soon.)

◇ **Date #5:** Three weeks later, you discover the person *isn't* better than nothing.

◇ **Date #6:** Three weeks later, the person wants to return to his or her ex. (You were used as a rebound once again!)

◇ **Date #7:** Three weeks later, you knew this person was someone else's version of heaven. Your friends and family recognized that your picker was broken and attempted to find "just the right person for you." Once again, *they* (not you!) were wrong.

◇ **Date #8:** Three weeks later, you discovered **The Suffocater,** who has smothered you, hounded you, demanded all your time, craved your attention, showered you with gifts, and shown you off. (You want to get an unlisted phone number, and moving to a foreign country sounds attractive.)

⬧ **Date #9:** Three weeks later—cha-ching!—the person's gone, and you're alone with an empty wallet or purse.

⬧ **Date #10:** Three weeks later, after discovering that only one of you believed in monogamy, you're wondering, "Which one am I?" (Take a number, please.)

⬧ **Date #11:** Three weeks later, you understand that physical attraction doesn't equal sexual compatibility. ("Spank me!" isn't a phrase you long to hear or say.)

If you're changing dates as frequently as you change clothes, find a better store, and start shopping when you have a clear picture of what you intend to buy. The object is to "buy" a healthy version of what you love, with no returns or refunds due to manufacturer's defect. After reading this book, buyer's remorse will be a thing of the past.

THE DESERT

The Desert relationship, like the terrain it's named for, is dry, dead, and barren. There was little sign of life from the beginning, but that didn't stop it from taking off and lasting for years. The marriage announcement should have read, "I did, I knew, I chose to ignore." Those who are experienced in multi-marriages will relate.

Desert relationships are futile from the beginning. Those who choose to be in one usually do so for the wrong reasons—obligation, expectations (family pressure), religion, fantasy (they'll change), debt, long-term co-habitation, or because you think that being good friends will make up for not being good lovers.

While Desert relationships tend to have some charm and perhaps some romance in the beginning, the climate simply isn't conducive for growth. At least one of your wells runs dry quickly. But instead of look-

ing for love and a relationship that could provide it, you'll stand at the dry well, hoping it will somehow fill. How long will you wait for the passionate love that won't come? How long will you convince yourself that you're doing the right thing by staying in a relationship that meets your external needs but doesn't give you what you really desire?

Our goal is to move you from the dry, desolate conditions that have drained your passion and into a hot, steamy, satisfying environment perfect for growth. A flower can't survive desert conditions for long, and neither can you.

Is Your Picker Broken?

All revolving-door relationships have one common denominator—people who do a poor job of picking someone else. The poor picking pattern is hard to break. It can only change when three things happen: You acknowledge your previous denial/mistakes/character defects and face what's happening; you become willing to change, and you learn why you pick poorly and how you can change your old ways. Once you "fix your Broken Picker," things *will* get better and you'll have a much better chance of finding the lasting love you deserve.

As long as you have a Broken Picker, you will continually repeat actions, such as attracting dead-end relationships. The situation may look different with each person you choose, but the same underlying causes and conditions that motivated your previous picks still exist. You remain hopeful that "This time will be different." We regularly hear people say, "I'm going to choose someone completely different this time" or "I refuse to date someone who's like anyone I've ever dated before." In reality, subconscious habit and emotional conditioning drive us to respond to what's familiar. Therefore, no matter how vehemently

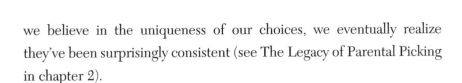

we believe in the uniqueness of our choices, we eventually realize they've been surprisingly consistent (see The Legacy of Parental Picking in chapter 2).

What's the difference between an abusive alcoholic plumber, an abusive workaholic doctor or a gambling-addicted businessman? While the three appear to be different based upon their financial, emotional, and social characteristics, all have addictive or obsessive-compulsive behavior that can lead to failed relationships. Interestingly enough, a woman whose picker depended on old, flawed data married all three and still complained, "How could this happen? I chose differently each time yet still ended up with the same results!"

> **66 All revolving-door relationships have one common denominator— people who do a poor job of picking someone of the opposite sex. 99**

From birth we're conditioned to seek what's familiar. Whether it's positive or negative, we become good at whatever we practice. You may have watched unhealthy influences in your immediate world (divorcing parents), observed failing relationships secondhand (friend's or neighbor's parents dealing poorly with their problems), or read media coverage of the cultural decimation of celebrity relationships (O. J. Simpson, Lisa Marie Presley and Michael Jackson, Madonna, Princess Diana, Dennis Rodman, Donald Trump, and countless others). Through innumerable sources, we've been indoctrinated to believe that failing in relationships is common, acceptable, and normal.

We've also been conditioned to believe that relationships are disposable or replaceable. Many believe it's better to settle for involvement in a poor relationship than to have no relationship at all. We convince ourselves that misery beats loneliness. We settle for the short-term relief that instant gratification provides—the one-night stand, the rebound, the no-strings-attached, sex-only relationship, or the liaison with an acquaintance to conveniently "accommodate" each other physically in an effort to alleviate loneliness. Using these tactics is like putting a Band-Aid on an amputation. Like the common saying, "The light that burns the brightest also burns the shortest," more often than not, the relationship that begins with the greatest sexual passion often fizzles the fastest. Quick fixes often leave us with lower self-esteem and greater feelings of desperation. Long-term commitments that we *say* we look for, *talk* about having, and *feign interest* in, continually elude us. And society in general hasn't set a good example (more in chapter 5).

Relationships in our society do not need rehabilitation; what's never been whole in the first place can't be repaired. You must *build a healthy foundation* from scratch, first clearing the old base that never was solid. Had your knowledge been sound from the beginning, you wouldn't be reading this book with such hope and interest.

What Makes a Foundation Healthy?

To get involved in relationships that are healthy for you and your potential partner, you must understand and embrace healthy expectations. During our seminars, we're frequently asked: "What is normal?" "What is acceptable?" "Am I so drastically different that it will be impossible for me to find a mate or even a date?" The detailed description of

work, love, and play below may provide you with a foundation or basis for what is "normal" and healthy, and lead you to balanced harmony.

WORK

Work is more than the ability to dress appropriately and show up several days in a row. It's your capacity to be self-sustaining, whether you work for someone else or for yourself. By age 21, young adults often have three-page resumes. If they don't, others may question why they're not reaching their "potential." The work ethic of showing consistency and loyalty to one company or career is waning. You need look no further than professional sports to see how common "job-hopping" has become. The "two years and a cloud of dust" mentality permeates our society. Executives jump from job to job and company to company out of fear, boredom, and stagnation or to pursue a temptingly dangled carrot.

Unfortunately, many bring this grass-is-greener mode of thinking into their personal lives, which can sabotage and undermine relationships. Relationship patterns, issues, and stresses infiltrate your jobs and vice versa. How can you maintain a long-term relationship on either a personal or professional level if you relocate every two years? How can you be effective if you're transferred just as you develop solid friendships and become proficient at work?

Companies often treat people as expendable; the reality of being replaced, transferred, or laid off looms especially large for single people. Families are given some consideration, but singles are often relocated with little concern for their personal lives. ("After all, transferring to Alaska is for the good of the company and for your career advancement.")

Companies are seldom concerned whether a single person is in the midst of a long-term relationship. When the company says "Go," the relationship often goes as well; or at the very least, the bond a couple has established is put to the test over money issues and geographic location, to the extent that one partner may sacrifice all to follow the other. A single parent may have the additional stress of relocating children and finding new schools, making new friends, meeting new neighbors, and managing custody arrangements in cases of divorce or "difficult" breakups.

LOVE

Love is a sincere *concern* for a person's spiritual, physical, and emotional needs, including (and especially!) your own. An important aspect of love is that you can't give away what you don't have. Many people are burdened with poor self-esteem and fear that loving someone else is impossible if they can't even love themselves.

> 66 Love is a process, not an event. 99

As adults, we crave love. As abused adults, living in the illusion of love often leads to being hurt. When we've been disappointed, wounded, or frequently abandoned, our concept of love and loving relationships becomes damaged or distorted and we often feel that love eludes us. Maintaining a continuous, healthy interaction can seem impossible to those who have lived in the shadow of abuse. In an effort to shield a wounded soul, many become emotionally unavailable or numb. You may become an emotional cynic, professing to no longer believe in the concept of love, and insulate yourself from the next potential source of hurt. The attitude "I can't find love. I can't get love, and even if I do find it, it won't last for long" is what we call the **Intimacy Defense Mechanism.** Love begins at home and starts with a healthy

sense of self. It's a process, not an event. Love isn't a person. It's a dream and desire to have passion and to be passionate. It's the security of a hug that is always there, much like the unconditional love of an old family pet that's always available. Love is familiar to some, alien to others. Just as you must practice being a friend to have a friend, you must practice loving yourself before you can love others. Many who have previously experienced betrayal and fear must *learn* to accept love from a healthy source. Victims, unfortunately, don't feel worthy of love; but they are worthy. *You* are worthy!

Love is not to be mistaken for lust, fantasy, courtship, a whirlwind romance, heat-of-the-moment passion, or physical infatuation. It is not to be confused with intellectual arousal, pampering, idolizing, or compliments. It's not an intense experience that happens as the result of unclear conditions or mental incapacity (such as being inebriated or stoned). Love is flexible and doesn't require certain actions or thoughts. It asks and answers. Love allows you and the other person to make mistakes, and is still there in the end. *Love accepts that the best you'll ever be is human and that's okay.*

Love takes responsibility. The five characteristics of love within a healthy relationship are *trust, respect, intimacy, passion, and commitment*. Love is *attainable* when you let it happen, is *maintainable* because you make it happen, and is *sustainable* when healthy characteristics are met. Even if only one of love's essential characteristics is absent, love will die. Without trust, love will question. Without respect, love has no boundaries. Without intimacy, you won't be heard or understood, and love vanishes. Without passion, love withers. Without commitment, love strays.

All these lofty ideals are what we dream of achieving, yet we may find ourselves disillusioned and feel we lack the healthy direction, drive, and support necessary to achieve consistent, romantic love.

PLAY

The word "play" comes from the Greek word meaning recreate, as in to create anew. Sitting at home in front of your computer, watching another movie channel (or video), or drowning out all conversation with one of your 150 CDs is not recreation. It is vegetation or techno-avoidance. Consuming alcohol to the point of losing control is even more unhealthy. Nothing new is being created. And in fact, some things are being destroyed.

We tend to isolate ourselves by finding amusement in activities that we do on our own—such as playing video games, surfing the Internet, or working out. Because we seldom get out and interact with other available singles, our interpersonal skills diminish. Our communication skills, which go unpracticed during solitary activities, don't miraculously appear in a relationship. What we fail to use and strengthen atrophies over time. Thus, while we may see or sense exactly what we want, we may lack the skills to achieve what we desire.

Fortunately we have sports leagues, camping trips, social events, special interest clubs, group travel opportunities, volunteerism, civic activities, and political and religious groups that do promote interaction, spontaneity, fellowship, and play. Involve yourself in as many of these as possible, as you will learn from each interaction and person you encounter.

Reading the Sunday newspaper together is not considered play. Vegetating in front of yet another movie or sporting event does not constitute play. While you may be undertaking these activities together, they promote self-absorption. Couples at play visit the zoo, take in arcades, or wash their cars together. They go out with friends and expand their boundaries. They dance in public (even if only they can hear the music). They sing along at concerts as they acquire or support each other's

tastes. They laugh. They smile. They touch and converse. They become students of each other's lives and make time to study together.

SABOTAGING YOURSELF

This book examines the mechanisms, characteristics, pitfalls, and shortcomings that have caused your concept of love to fade (if you even had one in the first place). A significant number of people with whom we talk inevitably want to know why they can't find love and why they continuously sabotage healthy love when they find it. Having a Broken Picker prevents you from choosing quality partners and getting into healthy relationships.

How do Broken Pickers get damaged in the first place? Through repeated relationship failures, you develop personality characteristics that subconsciously demand failure. Here are several analogies that may make this point much clearer.

1 **Think back to high school.** There was always one standout—a gorgeous, straight-A student, prom queen, and cheerleader who could date anyone she chose. The most recent news (ten years later) is that she's living in a broken-down trailer with her three kids after her husband ran off with their 18-year-old baby-sitter. The once-prom-queen is now spending her days munching potato chips, watching soap operas, and collecting welfare. She's at a total loss about how her life turned out this way.

2 **A young intelligent, attractive, and dedicated employee puts in countless hours trying to get ahead.** Two weeks before his annual review he begins showing up late for work, unshaven, disheveled, and dressed

less-than-for-success. He's half-asleep at his desk and extends lunch hours well into the afternoon with no excuse. While his work has been impeccable for nearly a year, just prior to his review everything is going wrong—for no apparent reason. Once again, he is passed up for promotion.

3 **A baseball player has a spectacular season going.** He's hitting exceptionally well, with timing so perfect he appears able to hit the ball blindfolded. In his next game, he gets up to the plate and strikes out, but doesn't think much about it. The next time he pops out. His third at bat, he grounds out. Finally, he strikes out again. He becomes so concerned about his average being affected that he tenses up. What was once a natural, automatic, and confident rhythm has become a painful, agonizing chore. The player is so consumed with the fear of failure that he has moved far from his comfort zone. Stress, anxiety, and a lack of confidence have become overwhelming factors to guarantee failure. In spite of his prior successful hitting record, he's now conditioned to expect failure.

4 **A burglar accidentally leaves his driver's license at the crime scene.** What do these four people have in common? They're subconsciously driven to fail (for reasons discussed at length in chapter 4). How do these scenarios relate to you and your life? How many times have you gone on a date, and were so apprehensive that you "blew it"? How often have you played out a scenario of failure in your mind before you even said, "Hello?" Prior conditioning made it easier to choose a poor relationship than a healthy one because you've done it many times before.

THE NATURE OF SHAME AND ABUSE

Why do men and women remain in abusive relationships, eventually break away from them, and immediately turn to another abusive one? People who find themselves in such situations usually have several dynamics in common. In nearly every case of abusive relationships, relationship addiction, co-dependency, counter-dependency, or inter-dependency, you'll find deep-seated roots of shame, fear, and trauma. These characteristics are usually connected to one particular incident—growing up in an unhealthy environment or having sustained exposure to an abusive relationship, for example. Frequently, an abused individual is referred to as having a shame-based, victimized personality.

People who operate from a foundation of shame usually do so to validate their feeling of "See, I'm no good." They've been abused either emotionally (love or attention has been withheld), verbally (berated, threatened), spiritually (their beliefs ridiculed, forced, or prevented—such as not allowed to practice their faith), or physically (they may have been beaten, sexually abused, slapped, shaken, raped). What is done to them can be so severe or chronic that they begin believing that this is how they deserve to be treated, and they become acclimated to abuse. We have defined three forms of shame.

EXTERNAL ABUSE

Abuse can eventually make you feel that having someone, even someone abusive, is better than having no one at all. As abuse continues, a person's self-esteem and self-confidence can get whittled away until they become so shame-based that they can't break the cycle. They get accustomed to living with pain.

As we witness this phenomenon, we can't help but ask this perplexing question: Why would anyone who is finally free from an intensely abusive situation immediately get involved in a new relationship or return to the previous abuser? The answer is simple. Mistreatment has shaped their personality and basic character. As a result, such people will continue to seek out abusive and unhealthy situations or even sabotage healthy relationships with family, friends, or colleagues to maintain their feelings of being a victim. The revolving-door relationship, whether old or new, is one result of the behavior we've described.

INTERNAL ABUSE

The second form of shame is Internal Abuse. In some cases, if you are shame-based and choose not to repeat external abuse, there is a propensity to continue the abuse by "beating yourself up" in one way or another. We isolate ourselves, abuse or depend on chemicals, mutilate ourselves, develop eating disorders or psychosomatic illness, become workaholics, and deprive ourselves of sleep, to name just a few variations we use for self-punishment and destruction.

THE SETUP

The third form of shame is called the **Setup.** Individuals who exhibit this form of shame have stopped external abuse, probably sought help, and recognize their various forms of internal abuse. Yet, because of their shame, these people take perfectly healthy relationships and sabotage them by not returning phone calls, being emotionally unavailable, and arriving excessively late for dates and appointments. A healthy person eventually gets frustrated with a shame-based person's

behavior and terminates the relationship. The shame-based person can then look at them and say, "I knew you didn't really love me. See, I'm no good."

Unfortunately, society doesn't provide easily accessible or affordable assistance to victims of abuse. In many cases, an appropriate treatment for each one is hard to come by. Shame is often systemically reinforced. It's not uncommon for these individuals to come from abusive family situations where relatives and friends support the denial and delusion that may exist for people with a shame-based victimized personality. The family feeds their denial. Employers may also be guilty of enabling employee denial. For example, rather than forcing employees to seek assistance or counseling for their problems, companies allow chronic sick days to pile up, and stress-related social life issues to permeate the workplace and affect performance without addressing them.

As mentioned earlier, fear is a topic unto itself. Experience has taught us that abusers and victims tend to operate out of two kinds of fear: the fear of not getting something they want or of losing something they have. Although there's a strong connection between guilt, fear, and shame, there's also a distinct difference that people regularly confuse. Guilt is usually a correctable mistake, such as feeling guilty about lying to someone before confessing. After telling the truth, you've cleared the wreckage and corrected the situation. Guilt acknowledges: "I made a mistake."

Shame is a validation of "See, I'm no good" or "I'm never good enough" and is chronically based in a person's character. These feelings are often blown out of proportion compared to the actual incident that caused the shame. For example, people who suffer abuse from a spouse or partner, despite physical and emotional damage inflicted upon them, will believe that "It was my fault" or "I deserved it. I brought it on." They can be manipulated into believing it won't happen again, despite this being their fifth trip to the hospital in the past three months. Shame believes, "I am a mistake."

FINDING YOUR WAY

As you read, think about these questions: When is a heart unavailable? How can I stop my attraction to those whose hearts are unavailable to me? Is my heart *too* available? What can be done to make the heart I seek more available? What will empower me to have the wisdom to know the difference? How can I use the tools found within this book to pick and sustain healthy relationships? *How can I date smarter?*

If you feel troubled after reading this chapter, chances are we struck a nerve and you can use some help. The more you discuss your past with healthy people, the more likely you'll be able to find ways to transform your old patterns into healthy new ones. Then you can begin to take an active role in developing the social life you desire.

> 66 Feelings aren't facts; they are thoughts. Change your thoughts and you'll change your feelings. 99

You *can* enjoy a healthy relationship if you so choose. Our book will show you that in order to find and maintain a healthy relationship you need to live in the solution, not wallow in the problem. It's impossible to focus on a solution until you know what the problem is and what caused it. You may feel that having a Broken Picker is a way of life; however, it's in fact a state of mind. Feelings aren't facts; they are thoughts. Change your thoughts and you'll change your feelings. You can resolve your past with **edu-therapy** (things you do on your own to

enact personal change through reprogramming yourself with new data), through self-examination, and by equipping yourself with indispensable tools that can fix your Broken Picker and turn your passionate dreams into lasting realities.

Now, let's find out what shape you're in. You'll discover that your current condition drives the choices you make and determines whether or not your picks will be successful ones. You're about to engage in eye-opening, innovative, and reliable exercises and techniques that will provide you with invaluable information designed to help you unload the baggage you've acquired over the years. Find your favorite pen, refill your favorite beverage, and let's get started.

Would You, Could You, Should You Date . . . You?

The tablets of stone—you know, the ones Moses brought down from Mount Sinai—clearly defined the rules for relationships and left little room for misinterpretation. Some biblical truths include:

◇ **Do unto others as you would have them do unto you.**

◇ **Honor thy father and thy mother.**

◇ **Thou shalt not kill.**

◇ **Thou shalt not commit adultery.**

◇ **Thou shalt not give false testimony.**

◇ **Thou shalt not covet thy neighbor's wife.**

Essentially, the big picture was for man and woman to get hooked up. Dating became the favored method after matchmakers lost popularity. From the time of the crusades, when relationships were arranged for property settlement purposes; throughout history when relationships were "bought and sold"; today where relationships are facilitated by newspapers, magazines, dating services, and Internet sites that dictate we find our soul mate—we date because society insists that we must.

Let's put rules aside and look at pure chemistry. Darwin's Theory of Evolution emphasizes our basic animal need for procreation. The bottom line is that we wouldn't be here if our hairy little ancestors hadn't let it all hang out. Some evolutionists theorize that by nature, we wouldn't know how to procreate if it weren't for the animals, that man is the only animal that needs to be taught how to have intercourse. In the twentieth century, we've taken our search for intimate relationships to the extreme. The statistics speak for themselves, as overwhelming numbers of people place single's advertisements, join matchmaking Internet sites, tune into talk radio programs aimed at the desperate and dateless, experiment with voice mail, explore video dating, and attend countless single's outings.

No matter what our personal preference or approach is, the truth remains consistent. As human beings, we're inherently lonely, crave affection, and want others to validate us through shared common experiences. Yes, we date because we have to, but we also date because we want to. Have you been searching for that special someone, for your "perfect" match or "soul mate," or for someone with whom to have a good time? Can't find one? Can't keep him or her? Do you wonder why? The answer may be found by looking at who you date and why.

❋ OBVIOUS AND NOT-SO-OBVIOUS REASONS FOR DATING

Why do you date? The most obvious answer is, "Because I'm attracted to someone." The actual answer, however, is not always as simple, positive, or healthy as you might expect. The following lists motives that may consciously and subconsciously drive you to date:

◇ **You date because you have a goal or hidden agenda.** You see a larger picture beyond dating—to find a long-term relationship and get

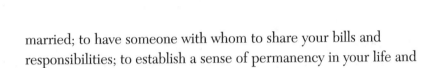

married; to have someone with whom to share your bills and responsibilities; to establish a sense of permanency in your life and get "off the market."

◇ **You date as a form of trophy hunting.** You search for the "hot babe" or "gorgeous hunk" who will look great on your arm and inflate your ego. You date for money, security, power, position, and sex. You date for the quick fix.

◇ **You date out of boredom.** You concede that even dating the wrong person beats being home alone . . . again.

◇ **You date to announce that you're breaking the bonds of your familial ties and creating a family of your own.** You attempt to show the world that you're desirable, available, and mature enough to handle a relationship of your own. You announce this by attending debutante galas, going to college, moving out, getting a place of "your" own, and becoming as self-sufficient and self-reliant as possible.

◇ **You date to resolve issues, both past and present.** You use dating to get revenge, such as entertaining a friend's former partner to get even with the friend for a past hurt, or to be spiteful, such as getting engaged to someone you know your family despises. You may even date someone you think might be able to "fix" you.

◇ **You date to "bait and switch."** You realize that one relationship is on the rocks so you begin dating a second person to ensure that you'll have someone to be with during the transition. This strategy, which allows you to avoid grief, closure, and completion, is a tactical avoidance of negative feelings and fuels the disposable relationship mentality.

◇ **You date to gain the limelight through osmosis.** You choose to ride someone else's coattails. "If I was dating him (or her), my popularity and reputation would skyrocket." You set your sights on unrealistic partners for a relationship and then fantasize that they're within your grasp, even if you have no means of realizing your desired outcome.

◇ **You date out of fear.** You accept dates that your friends arrange for you because they worry that you've been alone for too long. Your parents set you up because they're anxious to become grandparents, or they're concerned about your having someone to take care of you when they're gone "Boy, have I got someone for you!".

◇ **You date to test drive and compare.** You compare your dates to other people as a standard of compatibility. "I'm looking for someone just like my father, but nothing like my ex." "You remind me so much of my mother." "You're so different from anyone else I've ever dated."

◇ **You date to exclude.** You limit your dating to only those who meet your mandatory criteria for religion, looks, education, height, weight, professional position, social standing, skin color, age, sexual preference, children, or financial standing.

◇ **You date out of convenience.** You find someone who has similar work hours, lives close by, or is far enough away to minimize concern about commitment or the need to modify your lifestyle.

◇ **You date for personal enjoyment.** You look for someone who'll make you feel special, pamper you, be attentive to your needs, and help you forget about or resolve your shortcomings.

◇ **You might even date to find a good, cheap "therapist."** You take advantage of someone who'll listen faithfully, judge seldom, and expect little in return.

Now that you have a better idea of *why* you date, let's look at some reasons behind your choices of *whom* you date. You might see your decision-making process as an exercise in weighing various options that present themselves. For example, you might choose to date someone introduced by a friend or family member; be attracted to a co-worker or an employer who shows "personal" interest; receive a positive response from an advertising medium on dating; be contacted by a former love

who is interested in reinitiating your relationship; or meet someone at a social event or gathering. Or it may be pure serendipity. Inevitably, your desire to date and the options that present themselves leave you in a position of choosing between what's available to you, what you're willing to accept, and what you're looking for. In a nutshell, you're developing **Minimum Dating Standards.**

MOTIVES BEHIND YOUR DATE CHOICES

The driving force behind your decision to say "Yes" to one person over another is your perception of the benefits you'd gain through the relationship. Here are some of the factors that influence your decision.

◇ You may choose a candidate who's likely to help you resolve issues that result from incomplete relationships with your parents or significant care givers during childhood.

◇ You may choose the perfect person to let you unload the baggage of unresolved issues from past failed relationships in your effort to stop your pattern of poor picking.

◇ You may choose your only current possibility. You say "Yes" to less-than-your-ideal in the belief that dating someone is better than dating no one. Loneliness drives this decision.

◇ You may choose a person who can give you external gratification: money, power, sex, position, prestige, revenge, reputation, and so on.

◇ You may choose out of pure, physical chemistry. The person may be attractive, youthful, or "seasoned," and viewed by others as a showpiece or trophy that everyone desires. Because you feel admired for making this "catch," you disregard characteristics that would normally be a "turnoff."

- You may choose someone due to his or her persistence. Boredom may support your decision to give in. Pressure from family, friends, or colleagues might encourage you to accept an offer you're not wild about.

- You may choose someone based upon your own ethnic, cultural, financial, or religious practices and beliefs.

- You may choose a person you think is the opposite of your partner in a recently failed relationship.

- You might choose someone exactly like yourself in an attempt to match your likes and dislikes and avoid the "opposites attract" cliché.

While each is a common motive for selecting dates, we're sorry to say that none is healthy. When driven by a desire for companionship, we frequently lack the patience and objectivity necessary to select a partner for *the right reasons*.

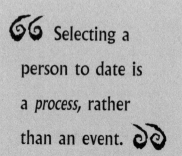
Selecting a person to date is a *process*, rather than an event.

Selecting a person to date is a *process*, rather than an event. If you understand the process you use to select a partner, you're more likely to base your choice on healthier motives and enjoy the fruits of better picking. We intend to provide numerous tools that will enable you to thoroughly examine why you date, why you make the date choices you do, and what the consequences will be. This understanding will help you get involved at a more reasonable pace that provides the opportunity to get to know a person better. Why subject yourself to the unpleasant results of bad picking when you can learn what you need to know before your lives become too enmeshed? This information will also help you to quickly see and eliminate a bad pick (more in chapter 6.)

❋ THE LEGACY OF PARENTAL PICKING ❋

Rockelle Lerner, a noted author and therapist with over 20 years of experience, has devised a simple test called "The Selection Process," to evaluate how you subconsciously select your relationship partners. We've adapted this powerful and insightful tool, which is easy to use and understand.

Upon completion of the exercise, you'll be provided with a thorough interpretation of what motivates your picks. The interpretation of your specific results will be unique to you. Please complete the exercise before reading our analysis so the results are accurate. Please read each of the four sections (A, B, C, and D) carefully and follow the instructions provided.

EXERCISE

ᏇᎧ

Picking Our Parents

SECTION A

Your Parents' Negative Characteristics

Instructions: Write down one negative characteristic about your mother and your father on each line. **Every line must be completed.** Even if one or both of your parents were "saints" in your eyes, they still had something less than positive in their character or behavior. It may be easy for you to identify the negatives (for example: "Mom was controlling," "Dad was alcoholic," "Dad was emotionally unavailable," "Mom was lazy."), or quite difficult as you view your childhood experiences from a different perspective.

List your mother's negatives   List your father's negatives

_____   _____

_____   _____

_____   _____

_____   _____

_____   _____

_____   _____

_____   _____

SECTION B

Your Parents' Positive Characteristics

Instructions: Write down one positive characteristic about your mother and your father on each line. **Every line must be completed.** Even if one or both of your parents were less than positive influences on you, they still had positive aspects of their character or behavior. It may be hard for you to identify these positives (for example: "Mom was a good listener," "Dad was a good provider," "Mom had a great sense of values," "Dad was home often," "Mom had a great sense of humor."), or they may surface quite easily.

List your mother's positives   List your father's positives

_____   _____

_____   _____

_____   _____

_____   _____

_____   _____

_____   _____

_____   _____

SECTION C

Positive Childhood Memories or Desired Positive Feelings

Instructions: When you think of positive memories from when you were under the age of 15, how did they make you feel? Please list the positive feelings you experienced from those memories. *If you can't recall any positive childhood memories, list feelings that you would like to experience today* (for example: happiness, love, feeling special, feeling important, feeling cared for). Make sure that you put one description on each line provided.

C. List positive childhood memories or feelings you desire

_____ _____ _____

_____ _____ _____

_____ _____ _____

SECTION D

Painful Childhood Memories: Survival Skills, Defenses, or Strategies

Instructions: When thinking of painful childhood memories, list survival skills, defenses, or strategies (for example: running away, anger, temper tantrums, hiding in books or music, lying, fantasizing, drugs, alcohol, food, humor, crying, sex) that you used to cope with your painful experiences. **It's very important that you put an answer on each line provided.**

D. List survival skills, defenses, or strategies you used to cope with painful childhood memories:

_____ _____ _____

_____ _____ _____

_____ _____ _____

How to Interpret Your Answers

The following section-by-section analysis is based upon the answers you provided. It will help you understand the motives behind the relationship choices you make.

Interpreting Section A

Take the sentence "I am looking for someone who is _____". and fill in the blank with the negative characteristics about your mom and dad that you listed in Section A. How often have you ended up dating (or even marrying) someone who embodied your father and/or mother's negative characteristics? ("You're so like my mother!" "You're just like my father!")

Examples for Section A:

1. I am looking for someone who is: (Mom's negative) *controlling*.

2. I am looking for someone who is (Mom's negative) *lazy*.

3. I am looking for someone who is (Dad's negative) *unfaithful*.

4. I am looking for someone who is (Dad's negative) *emotionally unavailable*.

When completing the phrase "I am looking for someone who is _____," with a negative characteristic, you'll discover that many of your answers will coincide with the negative characteristics present in individuals with whom you've experienced failed relationships. This doesn't mean that you consciously sought these characteristics in others; you probably just found a subconscious familiarity that mirrored your parent's negatives. In Interpreting Section B, we'll explain why this occurs.

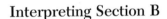

Interpreting Section B

Take the phrase "So that I can get them to be _____" and fill in the blank with the positive characteristics about Mom and Dad that you listed in Section B. How often have you wished that your unhealthy pick would exhibit the positive characteristics of Mom and Dad? ("You remind me so much of my father. There are moments when you make me feel special like he used to. You listen to a lot of what I have to say." "When times were tough, Mom used to treat me just like you sometimes do. She made me feel wonderful, in spite of it all. I could tell sometimes that she really loved and needed me.")

Examples for Section B:

1. So that I can get them to be (Mom's positive) *humorous*.

2. So that I can get them to be (Mom's positive) *emotionally available*.

3. So that I can get them to be (Dad's positive) *financially stable*.

4. So that I can get them to be (Dad's positive) *attractive*.

When completing the phrase "So I can get them to be . . ." with a positive characteristic, you'll discover that many of your answers coincide with positive characteristics you desired but were infrequently present in the individuals with whom you experienced failed relationships. Again, this doesn't mean that you consciously sought people lacking these qualities, but that you tried finding them where they were absent. You stayed in relationships too long, hoping these positives would appear, while the individual was unable, incapable, or unwilling to change. Fantasizing that the qualities you desired would materialize and become permanent kept you in an unhealthy relationship longer than you should have stayed. False hope in the individual's potential is the dangled carrot.

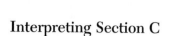

Interpreting Section C

Take the sentence "So that I can feel _____" and fill in the blank with the positive feelings derived from memories or desired feelings for today that you wrote in Section C (for example: "loved," "supported," "happy," "healthy"). These are feelings you're trying to recapture from your childhood or attain in your adulthood from lost-cause, dead-end, revolving-door relationships.

Examples for Section C:

1. So that I can feel (positive memories or desired feelings) *loved.*

2. So that I can feel (positive memories or desired feelings) *needed.*

3. So that I can feel (positive memories or desired feelings) *special.*

4. So that I can feel (positive memories or desired feelings) *secure.*

When completing the phrase, "So that I can feel . . ." with a positive memory or desired feeling, you'll discover that many of these memories or feelings were absent in your failed relationships. You overinvested in the relationship, hoping to experience these positive feelings when in fact you chose someone who couldn't provide them for you. No matter how much water you poured into your proverbial glass, it's still half-empty and you're still thirsty.

Once again, this doesn't mean that you consciously sought people lacking these characteristics, but indicates that you tried finding them where they were absent. You stayed in relationships far too long, trying to instill these positives in individuals unable or unwilling to change.

When you combine the answers from Sections A, B, and C, you'll find that you're "looking for someone who is _____ so that you can get them to be _____ so that you can feel _____." Revolving-door relationships reflect your unhealthy picking past. Practicing the selection process used in A, B, and C is your attempt to resolve incomplete issues

from your childhood or from behavior mastered during your revolving-door relationships. Your parents modeled your future for you, and history is repeating itself in your choice of dates. In short, you'll continue seeking out whatever you're familiar with. In a desperate attempt to complete, resolve, and conquer what did not work in your previous relationships, you'll continue to pick or maintain unhealthy relationships.

Looking at Section D, you'll see that the primary motives behind these picks are based on your self-sabotage of healthy relationships. Because they're unfamiliar, you tend to become bored, nervous, and frustrated. Sabotage becomes inevitable, leaving you looking back and wondering, "How did I let such a prime catch elude me?"

Interpreting Section D

Take the sentence "I keep myself from getting this by _____". and fill in the blank with the survival skills or strategies you used to cope with the painful childhood memories you listed in Section D. This section describes a person who is intentionally avoiding A, B, and C in a desperate attempt to attain and maintain a normal relationship with a healthy person. However, by performing the behaviors in D with a healthy person, you sabotage your relationships by subjecting healthy people to the unhealthy, unnecessary survival skills and behavior that you employed in your painful past.

Examples for Section D:

1. "I sabotage the relationship by *running away* or being unavailable."

2. "I sabotage the relationship by *not calling back and being excessively late for dates*."

3. "I sabotage the relationship by *making inappropriate comments, lying, and maintaining contact with ex-lovers*."

4. "I avoid communication by *hiding in television, as well as in Internet, books, and music*."

5. "Out of fear, *I have fits and tantrums to control situations.*"

In Sections A, B, and C, unhealthy motives and characteristics influence your poor selections. In Section D, it's probable that you've picked a healthier person, but you sabotage the relationship by acting out your own survival strategies. One way to improve your overall selection process is to be highly aware of the characteristics that you're subconsciously seeking in others (from A, B, and C). Learning to recognize unhealthy characteristics will enable you to practice the opposite behavior of what you relied upon in Section D.

This exercise demonstrates that you may have an abnormal response or reaction to a healthy relationship. By using the only programming you're familiar with—the defective one—you sabotage your own happiness.

Your discomfort in a healthy relationship may be due to a lack of experience or practice. Therefore, when you date healthy people, you tend to treat them as if you were still in an unhealthy relationship. Review the behavior you listed in D. You may notice that "the fish that got away" or the "nice guy or gal that slipped through your fingers" was probably run off by one of these characteristics, or you mistook serenity for boredom. A healthy relationship can feel boring when you're accustomed to chaos. So you create your own crises that not only sabotage the relationship but reinforce failure. Your ultimate solution for alleviating poor picking may be as simple as total avoidance—you avoid picking whatsoever. You can't go wrong if you choose to not select at all.

❋ COMMON EXCUSES TO AVOID DATING ❋

If you decide to abstain from dating, you'll come up with excuses to justify your decision. Below are the most common ones we've heard from people we've encountered. Are any of them familiar?

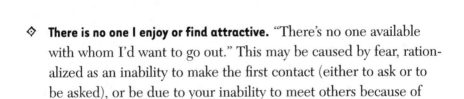

◇ **There is no one I enjoy or find attractive.** "There's no one available with whom I'd want to go out." This may be caused by fear, rationalized as an inability to make the first contact (either to ask or to be asked), or be due to your inability to meet others because of a diminished circle of contacts for meeting others.

◇ **I am in a transitory stage.** "I have to wait for the right time to date." You rationalize that you're moving, changing jobs, between significant others, only 10 years out of your divorce, or somewhere between failed relationship number 7 and 51.

◇ **The person I want is unavailable.** "The guy (or gal) I'm interested in is already married (or is committed) to someone else." "I'm in love with a famous person." (How many people can be married to a famous actor, athlete, or rock star at the same time?) It's difficult to date a potential soul mate who's already involved or will never be available to you.

◇ **Nobody wants me.** "What's wrong with me?" "Why aren't people I'm attracted to attracted to me?" "I always seem to pick people who are totally wrong for me." "I'm a loser magnet." You subconsciously send out signals that set you up to attract an unhealthy person or repel a healthy one.

◇ **I refuse to be hurt again.** "I'm angry and in denial, but I'll never admit it." "All men are jerks." "All women are gold-diggers and after commitment." Rather than risk losing again, you choose to simply not play! You use the memories of your past relationships as a rationalization for avoidance.

◇ **I'm broke.** "I am strapped and have little money or resources." You think you have to spend money to have fun, that time spent together must be occupied in some way other than just being together. You put more time and effort into disassociating yourself from a potentially great time than into using your imagination and finding inexpensive resources within your community to meet someone or make a great date happen.

- ◇ **I'm busy and have no time to date.** "Dating someone would decrease the amount of time I can put into my job (or church, fitness program, and so on) and I need to be putting in more time, not less." "It takes 70 hours a week to be successful in my field, and I want to be the best." What good is amassing a fortune, gaining great knowledge, or developing a perfect body if you have no one to share it with? All work and no play makes Jack and Jane obsessed, possessed, and dull—plus unlikely to meet one another.

- ◇ **I'm new to the area and don't know anyone.** "I don't have the desire to get out and meet anyone. It's easier to avoid the entire process." If you're unfamiliar with your new community, learning where to meet people may seem too difficult.

- ◇ **I have kids and nobody wants to take on that responsibility.** "It's hard to meet someone who would treat my kids properly. Plus, I refuse to allow my kids to get attached to anyone who might drop me. It's unfair to them." You assume that all potential mates don't want to date someone with kids, and you're concerned about the effect of your dating on your kids. You should also be concerned about how your children view your isolation, fear, insecurity, and excessive judgment of others. Children practice what's modeled for them.

- ◇ **I have no desire to date.** "It's simply not worth the effort, and I enjoy my life the way it is. Why mess up a good thing?" Your life movement pattern (daily routine) is comfortable, and you use not disturbing it as an excuse. Remember, however, that you could wake up one morning old, alone, without passion—and bitter.

- ◇ **I have not come to terms with my sexuality.** "My sexual predisposition is unclear so I am not sure who I should be dating, if anyone." No wonder it's unclear! Failure to participate fuels indecision.

- ◇ **I don't know whom to trust.** "Who is safe?" "Where should we go?" "How far and how fast should I proceed with the relationship?" "I refuse to be hurt again." Your fear of being hurt again makes not going out seem a better option.

◇ **I've been out of the loop.** "The last real date I had was when Moby Dick was a guppy." "I have no idea how to date in today's world." "I was never great at dating." "I am afraid of looking ridiculous and being embarrassed. I have no confidence whatsoever." Trying to date after being totally out of practice can be intimidating, but as with other skills, only through practice will you improve your performance.

◇ **I don't know how to ask or act when I'm asked.** "I don't know how to ask, and I'm afraid to ask." "I feel awkward and have no idea what to say or do on a date, if I even get one. I don't know how to dress." "I'm concerned their friends won't like or accept me." "What if I don't like the person? How do I escape?" "What if he tries getting intimate with me physically?" A lack of dating skills to protect yourself can keep you at home. (More on this in chapters 6 and 7.)

When you avoid dating for personal or social reasons, you may end up dealing with overwhelming feelings of self-doubt as you ponder what's okay, what to do next, what's acceptable, and how to re-enter the dating scene. You may have become so accustomed to being alone that the outside world seems alienating. The world may seem to have a perfect set of rules, that any unpleasantry, pain, or deviation from perceived norms will not be tolerated. Such discouraging feelings come from mistaken assumptions.

Attempting to live by unrealistic assumptions can cause conflict, chaos, a broken heart, or a lost soul. You may begin to believe you no longer control your choices because it feels like the world is beginning to make them for you. Through magazine articles, talk shows, and conversations with family and friends, we experience pressure to attain and maintain perfection at everything. The world seems to be judging you by what's outside, rather than by what's inside and your best intentions. (See Five Rules of the World sidebar.)

THE FIVE RULES OF THE WORLD

1. **You cannot have anything wrong with you.** "You must have the right car, friends, job, and money; live in the right place; live the right way."

2. **If you have something wrong with you, get over it quickly.** "We don't want to witness, hear about, or deal with your problems. We don't care."

3. **If you can't get over it quickly, fake it.** "Pretend, act happy, put on a happy face—show that you are F.I.N.E." (Ironically, this acronym stands for Fearful, Insecure, Neurotic, and Emotionally Evasive!)

4. **If you can't fake it and can't get over it quickly, at least have the decency to leave.** "Pain, pain, go away, come again some other day . . . but come back fixed."

5. **You can't have anything wrong with you.** If you do have something wrong, get over it quickly. If you can't get over it quickly, fake it. If you can't fake it, go away. Finally, if you aren't willing to do any of those, at least have the decency to feel guilty. Apologize for things that you have no control over.

(From Tom W. Lecture Colorado I.C.Y.P.A.A. 1995.)

The combination of unrealistic external expectations and internal remorse has left you caught in a double standard. You're trying to serve two masters: society's expectations and your own needs. The punch line to these rules is simply this: To get better you have to break all five rules! One way to conquer those rules is to improve your picking: You must recognize the causes, conditions, and characteristics that have caused you to maintain unhealthy relationships or sabotage healthy ones and understand why you let outside pressures block your progress. The Legacy of Parental Picking exercise focused on the motives for why you pick certain people. The Relationship Readiness Questionnaire will help you identify the characteristics and behaviors that keep you in an unhealthy relationship or allow you to sabotage a healthy one.

EXERCISE

∽

The Relationship Readiness Questionnaire

The purpose of this questionnaire is to determine to what extent you are experiencing and practicing a loving, meaningful involvement with others. Read each statement carefully, then decide which of the four word choices most typically applies to your entire relationship history (since you began dating). *Remember*: There are no right or wrong answers. Relax, think, and be honest!

Instructions: Write the letter that corresponds to the word you choose in the blank at the left.

A. Most of the time

B. Sometimes

C. Rarely

D. Never

1. Do you consider yourself to be a valuable person *without* a partner? _____

2. Do you feel greatly "improved" by an intimate relationship? _____

3. Do you value a relationship for its ability to make you feel more attractive or accomplished? _____

4. To what extent do you maintain serious outside interests which are separate from your primary relationship? _____

5. To what extent do you experience feelings of jealousy and/or resentment of a partner's outside interests which *do not include you?* _____

6. Are you friends with your lover/significant other? _____

7. Have you ever felt "compelled" to change your partner to satisfy personal needs? _____

8. Do you experience feelings of worry or anxiety when your partner tells you that they just met an "interesting" person? _____

9. Do you enjoy feeling "engulfed" by your partner? _____

10. During a relationship, have you ever maintained secretive involvement with another as an "insurance policy" against the primary partner leaving? _____

11. Do you believe that jealousy is a necessary part of loving someone? _____

12. Do you believe that the basis of a relationship should be to become as close as possible to the other person? _____

13. Do you trust your partner when it comes to loyalty/fidelity? _____

14. Do you find yourself getting involved in a relationship in order to fill a void or to escape loneliness? _____

15. To what extent do you feel "less a person" without a partner? _____

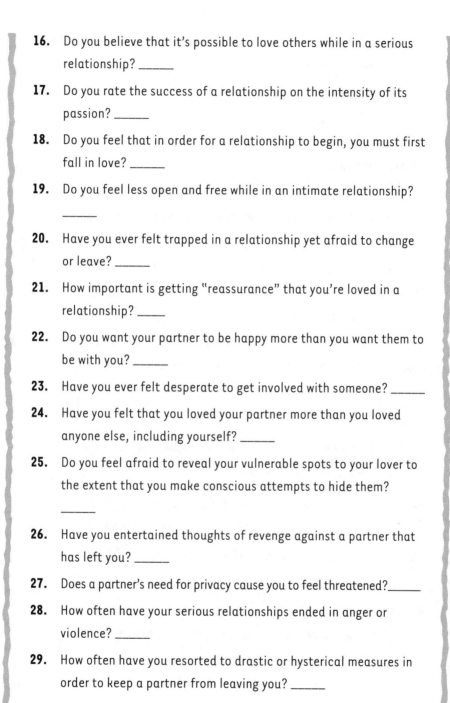

16. Do you believe that it's possible to love others while in a serious relationship? _____

17. Do you rate the success of a relationship on the intensity of its passion? _____

18. Do you feel that in order for a relationship to begin, you must first fall in love? _____

19. Do you feel less open and free while in an intimate relationship? _____

20. Have you ever felt trapped in a relationship yet afraid to change or leave? _____

21. How important is getting "reassurance" that you're loved in a relationship? _____

22. Do you want your partner to be happy more than you want them to be with you? _____

23. Have you ever felt desperate to get involved with someone? _____

24. Have you felt that you loved your partner more than you loved anyone else, including yourself? _____

25. Do you feel afraid to reveal your vulnerable spots to your lover to the extent that you make conscious attempts to hide them? _____

26. Have you entertained thoughts of revenge against a partner that has left you? _____

27. Does a partner's need for privacy cause you to feel threatened? _____

28. How often have your serious relationships ended in anger or violence? _____

29. How often have you resorted to drastic or hysterical measures in order to keep a partner from leaving you? _____

30. How often have your relationships involved chaos, violence, and / or emotional pain? _____

When you find out a partner's weakness or vulnerable points, how often do you feel

    31. Saddened? _____

    32. Irritated? _____

    33. A sense of power? _____

34. To what extent do you believe that you can't trust the people you date? _____

35. When having sex, how often do you initiate advances? _____

36. During lovemaking, how often do you feel that it's more important to satisfy your partner than yourself? _____

(Please rate *each* answer below.) When you learn of a new and different aspect of your partner's personality, how often do you feel

    37. Pleasantly surprised? _____

    38. Pleased, if it affects you positively? _____

    39. Worried about the effect on the relationship? _____

    40. Appreciative of their growth? _____

41. As a relationship progresses, to what extent do you find that your partner is very different than you had originally perceived? _____

42. To what extent do you feel that "you" should be your partner's best friend? _____

43. When a relationship has ended, how often do you allow yourself time to get over it and/or spend time "with yourself" before looking for a new one? _____

44. When a relationship has ended, to what extent are you fearful of becoming involved again? _____

45. When you feel that a relationship is "threatened," how often do you believe that you can save it by trying harder? _____

46. How often has open/honest communication been a part of your relationships? _____

How often would you say that you've been involved with kind and stable people, whether male or female friends:

47. Men: _____

48. Women: _____ (*answer both*)

49. To what extent is it important to you to know that your partner "Can't live without you?" _____

50. To what extent is "being loved" a primary goal in your life? _____

51. How often do you feel that your emotional needs were met by your parents/significant others? _____

52. To what extent do you feel that your emotional needs have been met in your current (or most recent/last) relationship? _____

53. How often do you feel that emotionally you "do most of the giving" in any relationship, especially your most serious ones? _____

54. How often do you spend time thinking and/or worrying about a relationship, either one you're currently in or one you hope to find? _____

55. To what degree is it important that a partner meet your expectations? _____

56. When separated from a partner for any significant period of time (i.e, business trip, extended travel, family crisis, etc.) how often do you experience anxiety, depression, worry, a diminished sense of self, or extreme loneliness? _____

How to Score Your Answers

Answer values are provided below for each letter choice. Write the corresponding point value for the answer you gave to each question. Please note that the point values for each letter are not always the same for every statement. For example, in statement # 1, A is equal to "0," whereas in statement #2, A is equal to "2." Add the point values for all 56 questions together to come up with your total score. Following is an explanation of the different scores.

Relationship Readiness Questionnaire Scoring Chart

Question #	Choices & Values
_____ 1.	A=0 B=1 C or D=2
_____ 2.	A=2 B=1 C or D=0
_____ 3.	A=2 B=1 C or D=0
_____ 4.	A=0 B=1 C or D=2
_____ 5.	A=2 B=1 C or D=0
_____ 6.	A=1 B=0 C or D=1
_____ 7.	A=2 B=1 C or D=0
_____ 8.	A=2 B=1 C or D=0
_____ 9.	A=2 B=1 C or D=0
_____ 10.	A=2 B=1 C or D=0
_____ 11.	A=2 B=1 C or D=0
_____ 12.	A=2 B=1 C or D=0
_____ 13.	A=0 B=1 C or D=2
_____ 14.	A=2 B=1 C or D=2
_____ 15.	A=2 B=1 C or D=0
_____ 16.	A=0 B=1 C or D=2
_____ 17.	A=2 B=1 C or D=0
_____ 18.	A=2 B=1 C or D=0

Question #	Choices & Values
_____ 19.	A=2 B=1 C or D=0
_____ 20.	A=2 B=1 C or D=0
_____ 21.	A=2 B=1 C or D=0
_____ 22.	A=0 B=1 C or D=2
_____ 23.	A=2 B=1 C or D=0
_____ 24.	A=2 B=1 C or D=0
_____ 25.	A=2 B=1 C or D=0
_____ 26.	A=2 B=1 C or D=0
_____ 27.	A=2 B=1 C or D=0
_____ 28.	A=2 B=1 C or D=0
_____ 29.	A=2 B=1 C or D=0
_____ 30.	A=2 B=1 C or D=0
_____ 31.	A=2 B=1 C or D=0
_____ 32.	A=2 B=1 C or D=0
_____ 33.	A=2 B=1 C or D=0
_____ 34.	A=2 B=1 C or D=0
_____ 35.	A=1 B=0 C or D=2
_____ 36.	A=2 B=0 C or D=1
_____ 37.	A or B=0 C or D=1
_____ 38.	A=2 B or C= 1 D=0
_____ 39.	A=2 B or C=1 D=0
_____ 40.	A=0 B=1 C or D=2
_____ 41.	A=2 B=1 C or D=0
_____ 42.	A=2 B=0 C or D=1

(continues)

Question #	Choices & Values
_____ 43.	A=0 B=1 C or D=2
_____ 44.	A=2 B=1 C or D=0
_____ 45.	A=2 B=1 C or D=0
_____ 46.	A=0 B=1 C or D=2
_____ 47.	A=0 B=1 C or D=2
_____ 48.	A=0 B=1 C or D=2
_____ 49.	A=2 B=1 C or D=0
_____ 50.	A=2 B=1 C or D=0
_____ 51.	A=0 B=1 C or D=2
_____ 52.	A=0 B=1 C or D=2
_____ 53.	A=2 B=0 C or D=1
_____ 54.	A=2 B=1 C or D=0
_____ 55.	A=2 B=1 C or D=0
_____ 56.	A=2 B=1 C or D=0

_____ Grand total for all 56 questions.

The closer your total score is to "0," the better your understanding is of loving relationships and yourself. A total score of 45 or higher may indicate a deficient concept of love (self and others), a lack of personal/interpersonal growth, or even compulsive/unhealthy behavior when relating to others. Please note that any question you answered that was valued at 2 points represents an area that needs attention and change.

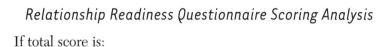

Relationship Readiness Questionnaire Scoring Analysis

If total score is:

0 to 25: Chances are you grew up with a healthy concept of a nurturing relationship. One or both parents (significant others) demonstrated confidence in their own value and self-esteem, and taught by example a fairly solid sexual identity. Chances are, there were few dependency issues. If this was your score, congratulations! You've learned the core of loving: it is healthy, giving, self-originated, and doesn't carry dysfunction as its center. People who score within this range will be unlikely to engage in revolving-door relationships.

26 to 50: Perhaps you have one parent/significant other who has a healthy self-concept. It's more likely that you grew up with a mixture of both negative and positive role models and some family dysfunction. You probably (and fortunately) identified with the healthier role model in order to have the concept of loving that your score indicates. However, you need to work on issues of self-esteem and being honest with yourself. Your score indicates that while you may understand what a healthy and loving relationship is, you don't practice these principles in some areas. In some of your relationships, you may find that you're seen as somewhat selfish or distant, two areas you'll want to be aware of. Keep growing and retake the test in a year!

51 to 75: You can work to change several issues. Your score shows a fairly heavy degree of relationship addiction/affliction as well as "co-dependency," which means that part of your character has become negatively influenced by exposure to someone else's unhealthy behavior. The dependent person responds to this behavior as if it were normal, participating in it as well. The majority of your relationships have probably been addictive or dysfunctional, rather than truly loving because your role models growing up were most likely addicted and/or compulsive. One parent may have been chemically dependent, which indicates the origin of your co-dependency. You may also have your own compulsions in adulthood. Being in a relationship is probably one of them.

If self-esteem is low, you don't have a true understanding of healthy interpersonal relationships. It's probable that you're willing to change and grow, which is imperative for letting go of the harmful and unhealthy behavior that caused you much unhappiness. It's also probable that you were abused, either as a child or an adult. Your score indicates that you may have been abused chronically or been a victim of an extreme isolated experience. Once you begin to learn how to love yourself, you'll be able to cope with and change your compulsive need for fulfillment by attracting unhealthy/needy relationships. Much if not all of what you believe about yourself and "loving" is the result of an unhealthy lack of nurturing that occurred in your childhood or adulthood. One of your most difficult tasks will be to *forgive the past* and unlearn what you currently believe about relationships, love, and growth. The apparent high degree of unhealthy family behavior and unhealthy picks that you experienced has left you the legacy of never truly feeling loved.

76 to 112: A score of this magnitude clearly indicates very unhealthy relationship behavior, a high degree of co-dependency, and other debilitating compulsions. You may be sexually addicted as well, which you should look at more closely. Your answers show a background of acute family dysfunction where one or both parents were either extremely compulsive or addicted. In other words, you grew up addicted/afflicted— without a balance or healthy role model to demonstrate clear sexual identity and positive nurturing. You also appear to operate from a **Shame-Based Victimized Personality** mode, believing that you're without value and choosing relationships that will validate this conclusion.

You have difficulty trusting others and tend to blame them for your unhappiness, while assuming an unrealistic amount of guilt. Since your self-esteem is critically low, you believe that your inadequacies contribute to everyone else's unhappiness. You vacillate between the roles of victim, persecutor, and, at times, martyr. Aware of your unfulfilled yearning for love, you're both unable to recognize a truly loving partnership and are confused about how to handle one if you do. Much of how you relate to others is based on loneliness and a desperate need to control present situations so you can conquer the past. You're familiar with chaos in your interpersonal relationships, no matter how *uncomfortable* this may feel. Conversely, you have an outdated idea of "romantic love," which can create the very behavior that's addicting. What was once embraced as the characteristic of true love (*shower* each other with love, give more gifts, criticize only in private, be generous with your body, apologize, apologize, apologize, *speak* the love words) is actually, at its core, possessive, obsessive, and addictive.

You haven't yet learned that *love is possible only when you reach out to another person from your strengths, rather than your weaknesses.* Focusing your attention on being loved is not the best way to attain it. If you're willing to change and take responsibility for your life and happiness, your path to recovery can hold untold blessings and peace of mind that you had not thought possible. When you learn the difference between love and addiction, you'll realize that you don't *need* another human being to serve as the object of your security. When you practice the tools of recovery, you'll find healthier ways to replace the desperate and frightening void that you've previously filled with unhealthy, abusive relationships and compulsive behavior. Then you'll know the serenity and forgiveness that come from nurturing your spirit, forgiving your past, and becoming capable of maintaining a healthy relationship.

If your total score and analysis surprised you, don't be discouraged. You're not alone. In reality, your sum is probably more common than unique. After facing this emotional self-analysis, you may have swallowed some hard truths about why your dates and relationships have been so unsuccessful. Remember that it takes two to form a relationship. So, not only is it probable that *your* picker is broken, you've been attracted to others whose pickers aren't working well either. (Misery loves company!) When individuals with broken pickers meet, the attraction can be so strong that it overrides logical thinking and common sense. You've been there before, yet you can't stop yourself from making yet another unhealthy decision. Having done this exercise, you've acquired more knowledge regarding the characteristics that contribute to your revolving-door relationships. Treat this awareness as your ally. It can help you catch yourself before you repeat an unhealthy behavior.

The more you live in the solution, which is the opposite of your old behavior, the more likely you'll be practicing healthy behavior to attain and maintain healthy relationships. This includes being able to identify a broken picker when you see or experience it. Following is a list of 50 Common Broken Pickers. Don't be surprised to find you've dated or exhibited more than one type. It's important to understand that while each broken picker is unique, many of them share qualities common to your own patterns of behavior. We call this **Brand-Loyal Bad Picking,** which means you repeat poor selections based upon an acquired taste or familiarity.

❋ 50 COMMON BROKEN PICKERS ❋

1. **The Panhandler:** You have a tendency to pick someone who is overly needy. They take regularly and give sparingly.

2   **The Pinocchio:** You have a tendency to pick others who have a very difficult time telling the truth.

3   **The Girdle:** You have a tendency to pick someone who strives to control you and all aspects of the relationship.

4   **The Raging Bull:** You have a tendency to pick someone who is possessive, jealous, and prone to outbursts of violence.

5   **The Joker:** You have a tendency to pick someone who turns everything into a laughing matter. They feign laughter in an attempt to avoid the truth or a confrontation.

6   **The Friend:** You have a tendency to pick someone who is there when you need them; who is willing to listen to whatever you have to say; who rarely judges or places pressure on you; but who will never give you a passionate commitment or the type of relationship you desire. You may receive an occasional "peck" or hug.

7   **The Lay Away:** You have a tendency to pick someone who only serves to keep you "off the market." You become close friends, have many things in common, but lack passion. You won't cross the line into any type of physical relationship. But those around you believe you're an item when you're really not, which can keep you from meeting an available person.

8   **The Stepping Stone:** You have a tendency to use people as a means to an end. They're not the person you're interested in, but you believe that by dating them you'll get closer to the person you desire.

9 **The Project:** You have a tendency to pick someone who needs to be "fixed" in order to be right for you. They have potential and could be molded into the "perfect person" *if* that one "major" character flaw could be changed. You believe you are just the person to make that happen.

10 **The Couch Potato:** You have a tendency to pick someone whose idea of a big date is another rented movie or the latest game on the tube.

11 **The 100-Yard Dash:** You have a tendency to pick someone who wants an immediate commitment. They move at the speed of sound and are intensity junkies.

12 **The Gold Digger:** You have a tendency to pick someone who has large amounts of expendable cash available, but little else.

13 **The Tease:** You have a tendency to pick someone who lets you look, ogle, spoil, pay, and enjoy their company. But they don't enjoy yours in return. You're simply a way for them to pass time and get the things they want. You might pay, but you're never going to play!

14 **The Analyzer:** You have a tendency to pick someone who questions your relationship to death. "Why did you say that?" "What did you mean?" "How do you feel about that?" "Why?" "Why not?" In their attempt to get close to you, they push you farther away.

15 **The Whiner:** You have a tendency to pick someone who is never satisfied or content. They are constantly complaining about the "miserable" state of their life.

16 **The Hot Potato:** You have a tendency to pick someone who is gorgeous, handsome, or sexy but has no intention of settling down, especially with you. They seldom stay with any person for long. In their mind, they're too "hot" to handle.

17 **The Dog Catcher:** You have a tendency to pick someone who flees at the first sign of commitment or if they sense a "leash" is about to limit their freedom.

18 **The Mugger:** You have a tendency to pick someone who constantly makes some type of physical contact. They may grab elbows, hold hands, or put their arm around you. They thrive on P.D.A. (Public Displays of Affection) and the more visible the better.

19 **Mr./Ms. Freeze:** You have a tendency to pick someone who is as cold as ice. No matter what you do, you can't elicit an emotional response from them. They make great morticians.

20 **The Archivist:** You have a tendency to pick someone who is constantly keeping a running tally of who's done what and who owes what. They thrive on gift-giving, but expect them in return, and can easily turn into the Martyr.

21 **The Milkman:** You have a tendency to pick someone who "won't buy the cow because they're milking it for free." A shallow individual is using you simply to satisfy their sexual, financial, or emotional needs. As long as they continue to have their needs met quickly and easily, they'll never fully invest in the relationship because they get what they want anyway. You're giving it up too easily. Remember: when the milk is free, some people become lactose intolerant.

22 **The Doberman:** You have a tendency to pick someone who is ferocious, hostile, aggressive, powerful, dominant, and confident on the outside, but insecure on the inside. They overcompensate for a damaged sense of self.

23 **M.A.S.H.:** You have a tendency to pick the walking wounded. You want to personally nurse them back to health, but it's like putting a bandage on an amputation.

24 **Narcissus:** You have a tendency to pick someone who is already committed to and madly in love with someone else—themself!

25 **The Taxi Driver:** You have a tendency to pick someone who is constantly watching the meter as if it were running. They make it perfectly clear that they have limited time to spend with you and you should be grateful for any that you're alloted.

26 **The Convert:** You have a tendency to pick someone of an opposing or different spiritual belief system than your own. You fall for them knowing that this issue will cause significant problems in the future— and it does.

27 **The Leech:** You have a tendency to pick someone who requires constant validation of how wonderful, important, needed, and special they are. As a result, they suck all the life out of you.

28 **The Fox Hunt:** You have a tendency to pick someone who loves the thrill of the chase but once it's over, has no desire for you at all. Once the trophy is on their mantle or the notch on their belt, they're gone.

29 **The Architect:** You have a tendency to pick someone who has his or her life diagrammed like the blueprint for a building. They manipulate every aspect to fit their grand scheme.

30 **The Bird Watcher:** You have a tendency to pick someone who pays attention to EVERYONE *but* you. They'll even tell you how beautiful another bird looks or how sweet they sound—to get your opinion and make sure you noticed.

31 **Mr. Nice Guy/Ms. Great Gal:** You have a tendency to pick someone who is mannerly and pleasant to be around. They're devoid of romance, have few social skills, and little confidence. But your fear of confrontation and sense of guilt is greater than your willingness to end the relationship.

32 **The Broken Tee:** You have a tendency to pick someone who looks great at the beginning, but snaps under pressure . . . never to be seen or be useful again.

33 **Ebony and Ivory:** You have a tendency to pick someone who views life and relationships in black and white. "It's my way or the highway." They have no color. No spice. No variety. They show no compromise or initiative. "Yes" or "no" are the most in-depth answers they'll give, with an occasional "whatever."

34 **The Magician:** You have a tendency to pick someone who simply disappears without a trace. They vanish from your life into thin air. No call. No reason. No closure. Just poof . . . only to resurface in the future as if nothing happened.

35 **Bull in the China Shop:** You have a tendency to pick someone who doesn't or can't adapt to social situations. You're embarrassed to be around them and can't clean them up to take them places. They talk loud in movie theaters to ensure that the audience is aware of what they think will happen next.

36 **The Bell Hop:** You have a tendency to pick someone who comes with so much baggage that you spend most of the time as their therapist. By the time the relationship ends, their dysfunction has rubbed off on you.

37 **The Dishrag:** You have a tendency to pick someone who only "uses" you if and when they need you.

38 **Daddy's Little . . . :** You have a tendency to pick someone who is warm, safe, comfortable, and childlike. It gives you someone to care for who cannot care for you equally in return. The relationship is devoid of passion.

39 **The Rose:** You have a tendency to pick someone at first sight who is aesthetically pleasing, smells great, and is a joy to be around. But once you get too close, you feel the "prick" of their thorns.

40 **The Ken or Barbie:** You have a tendency to pick someone who looks great on the outside, but is shallow, or even hollow on the inside.

41 **The Fire Hydrant:** You have a tendency to pick someone who is always there when you need relief. They expect to be treated poorly, placing you in complete control. You won't see them change or complain. They just take what you dish out and like it.

42 **The Jackal:** You have a tendency to pick someone who feeds on you when you're down, broken, and wounded. They stick around until there's nothing left.

43 **The Rabbit:** You have a tendency to pick someone who is so busy hopping from person to person, that they're unable or unwilling to make a commitment to you.

44 **Ms./Mr. Perfect:** You have a tendency to pick someone who exploits your weaknesses.

They revel in imperfections such as: appearance, weight, and intelligence, and never miss an opportunity to indicate what's wrong with you and right with them.

45 **The Ultimator:** You have a tendency to pick someone who forces the issue, making you feel responsible for the demise of the relationship if his or her conditions aren't met.

46 **The Purse Strings:** You have a tendency to pick someone who is controlled and manipulated by their family and their wealth. Their chief concern is what their family and friends will think about you.

47 **The Ferrari:** You have a tendency to pick someone who is extremely high maintenance. They look great on your arm, but you have to pay big to play a little.

48 **The Biker Wannabe:** You pick someone who is an executive by day and bad boy or girl wannabe by night. They attempt to buy self-esteem and an alter-ego.

49 **The Affair:** You have a tendency to pick someone who is already married to someone else. Heartbreak is evident; the challenge feels great; the results are devastating on both sides.

50 **The Crush:** You have a tendency to pick someone who fulfills the cliché "Love at first sight." They are the end all—be all. They're perfect—your ultimate fantasy—but they simply don't know you exist.

As you begin to address your motives for dating, your behavioral shortcomings, the characteristics of those you've picked in the past, and the patterns of behavior you repeat, you'll begin to see that it wasn't just bad luck or coincidence that led to your misconnections with others. Resolving these issues requires a multi-level and in-depth understanding of who you are. With each exercise you complete, in this chapter and those that follow, you'll gain substantial personal knowledge that will empower you to break the pattern of revolving-door relationships.

3

Let's Fix What's Broken

✳

Imagine you're the pilot of a jumbo jet with 225 passengers aboard, settled comfortably for a two-hour flight. After a smooth takeoff, the aircraft ascends to its cruising altitude. Thirty minutes later, you realize you're making great time but are completely lost. To make it worse, the navigational systems don't appear to be working, and you can't make contact with air traffic control. As you prepare for emergency procedures, you wonder how you'll find an airport at which to land safely.

Just like an on-board computer guides an aircraft, our mental programming (our Picker) guides our decisions. Defective equipment that doesn't completely function will result in less-than-positive consequences. If our Picker fails to work properly, this can lead to overwhelming feelings of hopelessness, fear, frustration, shattered trust, and in the worst of cases—death.

✳ OPERATING WITH A BROKEN PICKER ✳

The three major problems on the imaginary flight described above appear to be damaged equipment, deficient programming, and the

inability to communicate with air traffic control to maintain a true heading or land the plane for repairs. No pilot would attempt to repair an aircraft while in flight. The sanest course of action would be to land as quickly and safely as possible at the nearest airport. Like the aircraft and crew lost in flight, many of us operate in our relationships under similarly desperate, deficient, and misdirected conditions.

We pick people who aren't healthy and later find ourselves in dysfunctional relationships. A continuous stream of unsuccessful, dead-end relationships leads to one painful episode after another (as desperate daters and hopeless romantics understand too well). Add to these the occasional one-night stand, complete with the usual unpleasantness. At the end of these relationships, we feel used, abused, and confused. Your problem won't correct itself without new data, new equipment, and help from a qualified source.

Throughout our lives we're exposed to countless unhealthy relationships. We may observe them in our parents, neighbors, or relatives; we watch them on television and movies; we read about them in magazines and newspapers. Our everyday exposure can program us to accept unhealthy relationships as normal. This not only contributes to our Broken Pickers, but contributes to permanent personality characteristics that drive us to self-defeating behavior. We either sabotage a healthy relationship or maintain an abusive one because we've been programmed to do so.

No one wakes up in the morning thinking, "Gee, I'd like to be treated like a dog today." Nobody leaves work, walks into a party, and decides, "Ah, let me find the biggest jerk in the room as my potential mate." The behavior that seems to say such things is unconscious. Despite your best effort to change your approach to yield different results, the "computer" in your brain continues to process what's famil-

iar and send the same signals—it's the only programming your brain has ever known.

CHARACTERISTICS OF AN ABUSIVE PERSON

The simple tools we'll provide will enable you to work through your Broken Picker issues in order to create successful change. Even the worst-case scenario can improve if you're willing to try at least some of the solutions we will offer. Recognizing certain behaviors as Code Red Characteristics will help you avoid making or maintaining poor relationship choices in the future.

Code Red Characteristics are found in unhealthy partners and relationships. They are subtle, but can be easily identified when you know what to look for. They're frequently camouflaged by emotions surrounding courtship, such as infatuation, which leaves us dazed and rationalizing that

> 66 Dating smart doesn't include being dumbfounded or lovestruck. 99

"this time things will be different." Code Red Characteristics obscure signs that should be obvious. Dating smart doesn't include being dumbfounded or lovestruck. Feelings of infatuation will eventually give way to clearer images of reality. By knowing what to watch out for, you may never again find yourself dazed by infatuation.

The list of Code Red Characteristics (CRCs) will help you determine what needs fixing in yourself, and what to look out for in others. Learning to recognize CRCs can help you avoid another poor or painful

pick. Utilizing awareness of your CRCs will empower you to quickly determine whether a person is right for you.

It's vital that you understand you don't necessarily have to "bail out" immediately just because a person exhibits a few CRCs. Some people's issues may have been resolved through therapy, self-help groups, or long-term recovery efforts. *Should you choose to enter into a relationship with someone who has less than five years of recovery or displays CRCs they haven't yet addressed, a sense of caution and closer examination is warranted.*

Watch out for the Code Red Characteristics listed in the sidebar on page 66 as you observe others. Being aware of what constitutes an abusive person can keep you from repeating mistakes you've made in the past.

If you currently recognize four or more of the Code Red Characteristics in someone, this is a strong indication that the person is potentially unhealthy for you. If a person exhibits 8 or more of these characteristics and has not completed treatment to resolve them, choosing to be with him or her is potentially hazardous. If they have any combination of 8 or higher (current or past), you are potentially sitting across the table from the lead character in the next Stephen King novel.

At this point, you might be wondering, "How am I going to get this information?" Ask, and ye shall be informed. By nature, people love talking about themselves. Many of the CRCs can be rephrased into questions. For example: "In this day and age it seems almost everyone is recovering from something. Is anyone in your family recovering from anything?" "How is it that I get to spend time with you?" "What happened with your last relationship?" "How and why did it end?" "What qualities haven't you liked about people you dated previously?" "With your busy job, how do you find the time to date?" The key is to be direct enough to obtain a clear picture of the person's six primary rela-

tionships (see below) and the history that surrounds them, without being blatantly intrusive.

RELATIONSHIP ADDICTION

In theory, a person needs to balance at least six primary relationships (at any given time) to achieve a stable lifestyle. Those with *specific* problems that have to be worked on will also need number seven (see below). Relationships requiring balance are:

1. Relationship with self (time to read, work out, shop, pay bills).

2. Relationship with family (biological or adopted; brothers, sisters, spouse, children, mother, father, grandparents).

3. Relationship with employer (showing competence and consistency at work).

4. Spiritual relationship or belief system (church attendance, recovery programs, volunteer activities).

5. Friendships (outside interests that make you part of a community, including groups, clubs, activities, neighbors, sports).

6. Intimacy/passion/dating/sexual relationship/significant other or spouse.

7. Support group systems (self-improvement, self-help, 12-step recovery groups, Bible studies, therapy).

A healthy person balances these relationships, with moderate peaks and valleys. At times one particular relationship may require more attention. For a healthy person, the imbalance is often short-term and rarely hurts others. A person prone to unhealthy or addictive relationships will focus heavily on relationship number six within the first few

CODE RED CHARACTERISTICS

How many of these characteristics are familiar to you?

◇ **May abuse drugs and/or alcohol, past or present, or may be a "workaholic."** "I went through rehab three times, but I don't think I have a problem. I just like to party a lot." "I can see you for two hours this month. Want to do something then?"

◇ **May have unresolved issues of child abuse, neglect, or dependency.** "Sure, my dad beat me, but I didn't care about him anyway. Did I get help? No, he's dead now. I'm fine."

◇ **May have a strong need for power and control in relationships.** "It's my way or the highway."

◇ **May express suspicion, jealousy, or possessiveness.** A short leash or fuse shouldn't be confused with flattery. "I don't want other people to see you dressed like that."

◇ **May be easily angered, enraged, or prone to violent outbursts.** For example, may spend an excessive amount of time screaming at other drivers on the road. "I'll teach you to cut me off!"

◇ **May have a damaged sense of self-worth.** "If I didn't have you, I'd be nothing."

◇ **May be unable to relate to others or be emotionally insulated.** "You think it's awful that the child got murdered? Well, everybody has to die sometime."

◇ **May search for the "strong" woman or man who will make them feel "safe" and/or "fixed."** "I was nothing until you came along. Now I'm a new person."

◇ **May be incapable of commitment to only one partner at a time.** They indicate that their prior relationships failed due to "cheating," yet they've done nothing to work on the reason they cheat. It's almost a given that such people will repeat their cheating because they got away with it before. "Yes, I cheated and I'm sorry. Now let me back in."

◇ **May manipulate or pressure to get their way.** "If you really loved me, you would do this for me [sniff, sniff]."

◇ **May have very few, if any, close friends or outside interests.** If they don't like themselves, no one around them is going to like them either. "I like just being on my own."

◇ **May be given to minimizing, rationalizing, or blaming others.** "Your friends don't like me because I'm different." "*I'm* not like that. *You* made me hit you."

◇ **May exhibit inconsistent behaviors.** This includes mood swings and depression. They may get excessively kind and giving to balance out their abusive side. "I only beat you for your own good." "I can break it if I want to. Don't ever forget who paid for it!"

◇ **May deny the problem and the consequences.** "You deserved to get hurt because you pissed me off." "You think that gives you the right to leave? I'll show you!"

dates. Their other five relationships suffer or become badly neglected. While the attention you get in this type of relationship may feel good initially, the price you pay is usually living on a "short leash" with severe control issues. The following lists Code Red Characteristics that indicate when a relationship is grounded not on healthy love, but on addiction. (We define addiction as continuing to engage in an unhealthy behavior despite the consequences.)

EXERCISE

Relationship Addiction Checklist

Instructions: Check each statement below that applies to your current relationship.

A relationship is addictive when (This also applies to past relationship behavior as well, not just current.):

_____ It is used to escape loneliness, unhappiness, or fear.

_____ It exclusively claims (consumes) a person's consciousness.

_____ One or both partners are unhappy or discontent with themselves.

_____ The relationship is used to fill a void.

_____ Constant exposure to the other person is necessary to make life bearable.

_____ There's a need to participate in every aspect of the other person's life.

_____ The individual feeling of identity (wholeness) is dependent on the approval and complete acceptance of the other person.

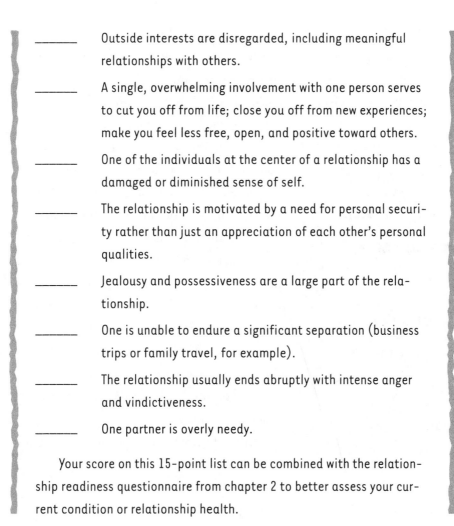

_____ Outside interests are disregarded, including meaningful relationships with others.

_____ A single, overwhelming involvement with one person serves to cut you off from life; close you off from new experiences; make you feel less free, open, and positive toward others.

_____ One of the individuals at the center of a relationship has a damaged or diminished sense of self.

_____ The relationship is motivated by a need for personal security rather than just an appreciation of each other's personal qualities.

_____ Jealousy and possessiveness are a large part of the relationship.

_____ One is unable to endure a significant separation (business trips or family travel, for example).

_____ The relationship usually ends abruptly with intense anger and vindictiveness.

_____ One partner is overly needy.

Your score on this 15-point list can be combined with the relationship readiness questionnaire from chapter 2 to better assess your current condition or relationship health.

How to Score the Relationship Addiction Assessment

If you or your partner are experiencing 1 to 5 of these characteristics, it's highly likely that your relationship will be sabotaged by unresolved issues or by your divulging too much information too quickly along with an excessive investment of time and energy. If 6 to 10 of these characteristics are present, this indicates that a serious relationship addiction exists and that your ability to successfully and painlessly terminate the relationship is unlikely. Professional help or termination of the relationship is strongly recommended at this point. If 11 or more characteristics are present, your future is predictable: intense pain, resentment, low self-esteem, fear, distrust, misery, and self-doubt. Recommendation: Run! Get therapy quickly!

> 66 What was abnormal can seem normal to you as you get used to living with it, making it difficult to recognize as unhealthy. 99

A major problem we observe is that people from addicted relationships transfer their intense neediness into new relationships. They come on too fast, demand too much time and attention, and overwhelm the other person with their need for instant love and gratification. For them, it's a matter of love on demand.

Inevitably, without specific treatment and a course of action, relationship addiction will consume you. If a high number of these characteristics are currently present in your relationship, you may be blinded or in denial. The tolerance you've developed to cope with dysfunction is a defense against facing what you're putting up with. What was abnormal can seem normal to you as you get used to living with it, making it difficult to recognize as unhealthy.

In many cases, we find extreme solutions to cope with an extreme dysfunctional history. We might go for months, or even years, without dating or seeking meaningful contact. On the other end of the spectrum, some of us find it traumatic to go for even a day without having some-

one care about us, or without having someone to care about. These extremes represent opposite sides of the same coin—a person who craves yet is afraid to express love (and might even be incapable of feeling it). These individuals are often so damaged at their core that shame, fear, and loneliness blind them from seeing the truth about someone with whom they want a relationship, no matter how obvious the warning signs are or who alerts them. How many times have friends warned you that someone wasn't good for you? How many times have you looked back at relationships and realized you knew the person was going to hurt you long before he or she did? How many times have you crossed back over "burned bridges," only to find the unhealthy person you left was exactly the same as before? How long will you keep convincing yourself, "This time it will be different?"

THE PERPETUAL LIAR

Why don't lessons of the past sink in? The old cliché says this: "Love is blind; but deaf, dumb, and stupid run a close second, third, and fourth." If you're thinking with your heart, rather than using you brain or even your gut instincts, you're not thinking at all. Thinking with your heart is responding purely from emotions. Your ability to hear, see, or believe the truth is suppressed by your desire to fill a relationship void. (Even misery beats loneliness!) We have a useful tool to help you sort the facts from the fiction that your wishful thinking may have created— a list of common behaviors associated with dishonesty. Lying is the primary tool of an abuser, and abusers learn to use it well. No one is perfect. But when it becomes necessary to keep a score card in order to separate the truth from fabrication, it's a sign to consider keeping better company.

How to Spot Liars in Action

Liars will:

⬦ **Avoid eye contact with you.** If they do establish eye contact, it will be for a very short duration and they'll immediately look down or away.

⬦ **Appear nervous and preoccupied.** They may stutter, fidget, switch topics in mid-sentence, swing their legs and feet, tap their fingers or feet, and exhibit rapid or severe mood swings.

⬦ **Overexplain or overjustify their version of "the truth."** A yes or no answer becomes a short novel.

⬦ **Change the facts and details of their story over time.** Look for quantity changes (such as a detail goes from "three days" to "a week" or "$100" to "$500"). You've heard about the fish that grew and grew each time "the fish tale" was told. The more time that passes between asking them questions, the greater the chance the specifics of their story may change.

⬦ **Modify the story to fit the circumstance or the person with whom they're communicating at the time.** They may tell one version to their wife and another to their child. When the wife and child compare stories, the central issues remain the same but the specifics are completely different.

⬦ **Change their style of communication.** An excessively verbose person may become quiet. A quiet person may ramble on. Depending on which gender they're speaking to, their story may vary. A frantic, panicky, intense story may turn into "how well I handled it," or a calm situation becomes a major crisis. One minute they're telling a first-party story—the next a second-party one. (The main character of the story goes from "I" to "He." "I heard" changes to "A friend of mine told me.") Liars look for the reaction they desire and will try different tactics to achieve it.

◇ **Answer your questions with defensive or evasive questions.** You might ask, "Where were you last night?" and get "Why do you ask?" You ask, "I thought that you just used my car to run a short errand. Why are there 100 more miles on it?" and get "Don't you trust me?" They always have an answer but it's never directed to the question you asked.

◇ **Probe for information, how you know it, and your source of knowledge.** "What do you think happened?" "Did you know that, too?" "How did you find out?" "You're going to believe them over me? Look how messed up they are." "What did you expect me to do?" They'll do anything to discredit your source and confuse you.

◇ **Become angry and defensive at being questioned.** "Who are you to question me?" "That's none of your business." "What gives you the right? You think that you know everything, don't you?" They try to stop your questions by putting you on the defensive.

◇ **Develop "selective hearing."** They hear only what they want to hear, what they want to respond to, or what won't cause a conflict of interaction. There's a difference between the truth, the facts, and the perception. The truth and facts get lost when their perception is all they choose to know.

◇ **Practice premeditated lying.** They calculate and plot strategies for deception. They constantly check on the schedule and where-abouts of the person they're deceiving to ensure a successful lie. "Can I get away with it?" "Can I get someone to cover for me?" They knowingly and unknowingly involve others in their decep-tion. They make you feel at fault for the miscommunications, mis-understandings, and misinterpretations as a ploy to manipulate your sense of reality.

◇ **Attempt to laugh off their deception as a joke.** "You've got to be kid-ding." "I was just trying to fool you." "Can't you take a joke?" They use inappropriate laughter and practice insensitivity. Ridicule and sarcasm become their normal tone.

◇ **Avoid you.** If they avoid you, their chances of being questioned and caught in a lie diminish greatly. They hide because they've been caught. They change their daily movement pattern. They make up stories about why they can't go certain places, attend events, or come in contact with certain people.

All the Code Red Characteristics introduced in this chapter are designed to prevent you from getting into yet another relationship due to a bad choice or decision. We want to equip you with awareness, but not paranoia. Your awareness may allow you the consistent recognition to sort through the unhealthy choices by which you may be tempted. These tools aren't meant to replace your emotional judgment, but they can enhance your ability to pick quickly and wisely.

We need to find the origin of our Broken Pickers and not fall into the trap of fixing the symptoms on a case-by-case basis. Many abusive and unhealthy partners have played the game for so long, and their skills of deception are so well honed, that they can easily escape and evade even a professionally trained eye. Our belief is that you need to be working on yourself as you become aware of others since you'll rarely, if ever, attract anyone healthier than you are. If you do, the attraction won't last long. Once healthy people begin to perceive that they're becoming your mother, father, brother, sister, or therapist, they'll disappear.

After digesting this chapter, you'll be ready to look for innovative ways to fix your Broken Picker and make healthier relationship choices. You're now equipped with precision tools that can help you intercept unhealthy relationships at their onset and rehabilitate your Broken Picker. These tools may also send distress signals that alert you when you're in an unhealthy relationship and in need of help. Your own dysfunction and numbness may have prevented you from seeing just how serious your present situation is. The information we've provided so far is not enough to overpower or replace years of prior conditioning. You'll

need to further investigate and educate yourself to realize permanent, consistent, and healthier relationship choices.

While achieving a safe landing temporarily alleviates a crisis situation, the faulty and damaged equipment must be fully repaired for successful flights to occur in the future. In the following pages, we'll examine various conditions that prevent your wounds from healing. Although the journey thus far has been rather turbulent, by the time you're back on course in chapter 7, the in-flight movie will be showing *your* "Love Story"—the romance you've always envisioned.

4

Why Your Relationships Are Like a Revolving Door

It was Ethel's turn to host the "Fab Five"—herself, Thelma, Velma, Bertha, and Eunice—for their weekly dinner "date." The five had met at a singles' function and became close, as all had one thing in common: chronic failure in relationships. The topic again this week (as if there were any other to discuss) was men.

To get things started, Ethel threw out the question, "Did anybody find a love life this week?" It didn't take long before each chimed in to describe her most recent failure, which was expected at each meeting. Velma responded first, complaining that her abusive mother had left her weekly sarcastic message reminding Velma that at least she wasn't alone when she was married to her second husband, Bill, even though he was an alcoholic. Velma then asked a question that sounded more like a statement: "There can't be many alcoholics left in this city for me to date, can there?"

Thelma eagerly commented, "At least you don't have to share your date with your sister. She has slept with every guy I've ever dated!

Bertha chronicled the various people who had tried to fix her up during the week. Her parents informed her that at their diet center meeting they met a nice, unemployed man with plenty of time to date. Her closest friend at work insisted Bertha go bar-hopping with her to meet a man, saying: "Just because you got taken advantage of once doesn't mean it will happen again." The rest of the Fab Five could see that Bertha was paralyzed with fear and wouldn't accept a date with anyone for any reason.

Eunice stated that she got a new job and that her boss was rich, handsome, intelligent . . . and married. That hadn't stopped him from making two offers to her already. The first was a nice promotion if she were willing to bend over backwards and put in some "personal over-time." The second was a transfer to a better job in another division so they could "see" each other. A few of the Fab Five members immediately offered that she could probably get him away from his wife. "If he were truly happily married, he wouldn't be pursuing you," they told Eunice.

Everyone in the room could practically hear Ethel's biological clock ticking and knew what was coming. She admitted that her parents had called, as they did every week, to remind her that they weren't getting any younger and wanted to be grandparents before they died and prior to the next millennium. Ethel, like the others, felt frustrated, confused, abused, and resigned to the fact that she saw no positive end in sight.

For the next hour, as they did every week, the Fab Five did their best to make each other feel accepted, valuable, and supported, but never addressed why the same issues kept coming up.

It's natural to protect ourselves from getting hurt in a relationship. When we've had a bad experience, some of us will do anything to prevent another painful one from occurring. You've probably turned to a defense or two (or perhaps more than a few!) to avoid setting yourself up for failure again. The trouble is that the baggage you carry into present relationships from past ones can keep you from getting involved with someone healthy.

In previous chapters, we examined our "Pickers" and the components we use to choose potential dates or mates. In this chapter, we'll explore the personal characteristics and old wounds that may lead you to sabotage healthy relationships or cause you to repeat unhealthy mistakes. The information below, though a bit "heavy," is critical to your understanding of the different dynamics that affect your behavior. Once you understand what may have prevented you from attracting (or being attracted to) the right person in the past, you can move in the direction of a healthy relationship. Slowly absorb the information we provide here. Look for potentially destructive patterns in yourself and in your potential partners. When you identify a behavior that applies to you, you'll be able to use the tools offered in the rest of the book to correct it. If you put in the effort to become a healthy person yourself, you'll be able to enjoy a healthy, happy relationship!

> **❝ If you put in the effort to become a healthy person yourself, you'll be able to enjoy a healthy, happy relationship! ❞**

THE 20 DEADLY SINS OF SELF-SABOTAGE

The "Fab Five" collectively suffer from what we refer to as the **20 Deadly Sins of Self-Sabotage,** feelings and behaviors we use to undermine our own relationships. We do this in response to fear, to protect ourselves from being hurt, or to defend ourselves against potentially abusive situations. Rather than resolving a problem and moving on, we temporarily protect ourselves by unhealthy means. The trouble is, they don't help in the long run. Although we might feel the "relief" these means initially provide, repeated usage can damage how we interact with people and how we feel about ourselves.

Review the **20 Deadly Sins of Self-Sabotage** below and try your best to identify which, if any, apply to you or people with whom you're involved now or in the past. Identifying a problem is the first step toward healing it; and once healed, you will attract healthier people and maintain much sounder relationships. Be honest with yourself as you peruse the list below. *Name* your problems, *claim* them, *deal* with them, and then *move on!*

1   **Jealousy and Mistrust:** Out of intense fear of losing your partner, you become jealous, believing they are attracted to someone else. This suspicion can carry over into future relationships and remain active years after an incident has occurred. Those experiencing jealousy and mistrust have an intense desire to know everything in detail, but rarely find any answers acceptable. Even confessions by the guilty party seldom provide you with a sense of satisfaction. A relationship can't thrive if one partner is always on the defensive. You may even catch yourself saying something like, "If you hadn't cheated on me ten years ago, I wouldn't have to call you six or seven times a day to make sure that you aren't doing it again."

2   **Confabulation:** This is lying to the point where you believe your own lies and get tangled in unnecessary webs of deception. You're frequently so convinced by your own lies that others begin to believe them, too. Lying destroys the foundation of trust in a relationship as neither party can tell whether a statement is fact or fiction and thus must render most comments meaningless.

3 **Possession-Obsession:** This "I want, I need, and I must have—exclusively!" mentality can lead to the suffocation of your partner. You think you love someone so much and find them "so perfect" for you that you smother them until they want or need to escape your overwhelming neediness. This pressure comes from what we refer to as Front Load–Overload–Burnout. You want too much, too fast, too often. Your need to share every aspect of your partner's life can limit his or her normal interaction with family, friends, relatives, and colleagues. It's hard for a relationship to survive when neither partner has a life apart from the other.

4 **Compulsivity:** This is a chronic drive, infatuation, or obsession to take a normal action and repeat it until it becomes unhealthy. It also motivates us to act on our desire for satisfaction and instant gratification. "I'll have one. Better make that two. Oh, heck, as long as I'm here, make that three."

> **66** Making the same pick on a different day will bring you the same problems on a different day. **99**

5 **Repetition:** This is entering, closing, and re-entering a poor relationship with the same person, despite the consequences and the predictable outcome of failure. Logic and reason elude you, thus convincing you that "I've changed; this time I know what to look for." "You promised it would be different this time." How many black eyes or disappointments will it take before you learn? Making the same pick on a different day will bring you the same problems on a different day.

6 **Rationalization:** When we manipulate thoughts, actions, motives, or facts to justify a wrongdoing or unhealthy, disruptive, or controlling behavior, we are rationalizing. It is the continued justification of an unhealthy behavior or bad decision. "He's never hit me before, but lately his job has been so stressful." Rationalization prevents you from facing the reality of your behavior and accepting the fact that you shouldn't be in a particular relationship. Remember this: whenever you say the word "but," an excuse is about to follow.

7 **"Justifiable" Blaming:** "Justifiable" blaming is failing to take responsibility for doing something wrong by accusing another person. "If you hadn't looked at other men, I wouldn't have had to sleep around." "I lied because you lied to me first." You point your finger at someone else to justify your wrongdoing. Conversely, by accepting the blame for someone else's unhealthy behavior, you cosign that behavior. "I realize that you went out with my brother to make me jealous because I spent too much time talking to that girl at the bar."

8 **Denial:** Denial is the disregard of facts, opinions, and information despite evidence to the contrary. If you deny problems and put up a façade indicating that everything is wonderful, you don't have to face them. Despite warnings from those concerned about you, it feels safer for you to deny the problems than to deal with them. It protects the sanctity of your dysfunctional relationship, and keeps you firmly entrenched in it. "Just because my boyfriend got his fourth DUI this weekend doesn't mean he has a problem with drinking. The police are just picking on him." Yeah, right.

9   **Gullibility:** Gullibility is the sincere desire to believe what you're told, despite the source and lack of facts. "Just because he's been married five times doesn't mean it won't work with me." In some cases, naiveté can be partially to blame. "She told me she was on birth control." A desperate need to believe can cause you to ignore the truth, no matter how painful it may be. "He said he'd leave her for me!" Gullibility won't keep the truth about your relationship from making you unhappy.

10   **Crisis Mismanagement:** This form of self-sabotage involves misreading minor cues and turning them into catastrophic events. Crisis mismanagement makes you feel useful and needed as you elicit feelings of empathy and sympathy, but it can cause extreme emotional swings and make every task seem overwhelming. How many times have you seen someone devastated over the loss of a friendship or relationship only to find out later that he or she was barely (if at all) acquainted with the person?

11   **Anxiety Prone:** People who are anxiety prone are driven by fear and need everything done immediately ("Right now!"). Their anxiety creates an overblown sense of responsibility and doom, and is frequently accompanied by psychosomatic symptoms of stress such as migraines, high blood pressure, irritable bowel syndrome, and skin irritations. The additional stress created by anxiety can put too much stress on your relationship. We're sure you know at least one hypochondriac—you know, people who are so wound up that they are almost constantly sick, even "dying," and go from doctor to doctor fearing the worst, only to be told they probably had heartburn. They keep everyone on "alert" with a bigger-than-life sense of urgency that everything must be done "now"—just in case.

12 **Mis-Prioritizing:** This inability to appropriately balance outside activities with the responsibilities of your relationship can cause you to place items that require immediate attention at the bottom of your list while you move insignificant, diversionary activities to the top. This defense mechanism helps you avoid your responsibilities as you give minor events, tasks, and situations more importance than they deserve. For example, you may surf the Internet at work instead of doing your job, thus risk getting fired. Softball games may become more important than significant others' birthdays. You may give in to your sexual desires without taking the proper precautions to prevent pregnancy or disease. Having a healthy relationship can sink to the bottom of your list, thus leaving you with dissatisfied partners or repeated broken hearts and dead-end romances due to neglect.

13 **Suppression:** Attempting to control, dominate, or manipulate others by disregarding their feelings, opinions, wants, and needs is the epitome of selfishness. Suppression includes all tactics you employ to stay in control and keep another person down. Guilt, game playing, criticism, anger, emotional withdrawal, and abuse are a few of the techniques you may use to secure your position and increase power in a relationship.

14 **Revenge:** Revenge is looking to make yourself feel better by hurting someone who has previously hurt or disappointed you. It is consciously inflicting injury of an equal or greater degree on someone who wronged you for the purpose of absolving your own pain. For example, you might pay too much attention to someone at a party in order to make your current significant other jealous because he or she did something you didn't like.

15 **Instant Gratification:** A quick fix to satisfy an emotional, physical, psychological, or spiritual emptiness or craving, instant gratification is usually an impulsive action that doesn't take into account the long-term effects. A need for this short-term happiness can lead to unhealthy actions resulting in long-term addiction, regret, and pain. You may turn to rebound dating, compulsive spending, a one-night stand, a vengeful fling, or soothe yourself with food when you're not getting satisfied in a relationship.

16 **Victim-Martyr:** You may subtly or openly use self-defeating behavior to validate your feelings of shame ("See, I'm no good") by playing Victim-Martyr. You get involved with the problems and chaos of other people's lives to deflect attention from yourself, and see yourself as being taken advantage of ("Used and abused"). Playing Victim-Martyr leads to a need to control a relationship under the guise of being "helpful." Victims cry wolf and complain vigorously about how bad they are being treated in a relationship while Martyrs stay in the relationship because they rationalize that they are needed, indispensable, and claim to be in control and helpful at their own expense.

17 **Distancing:** Distancing is communicating or behaving in a manner that prevents or discourages people from becoming emotionally close to you. You rarely return phone calls, have difficulty receiving gifts or compliments, appear withdrawn at social gatherings, and frequently won't engage in conversations or activities, even when encouraged. A relationship can't grow if one or both partners are emotionally unavailable.

18 **Compromised Loneliness:** Compromised Loneliness is the willingness to "settle" for a relationship with someone you would normally

never consider. Basically, you choose an unacceptable partner over loneliness.

 Emotional Paralysis/Analysis Paralysis: Emotional Paralysis/Analysis Paralysis is the inability to move forward because of unresolved pain or intense fear. After consistently being subjected to negative experiences on all levels, you may give up any desire to improve or achieve. Any chance of a relationship gets tangled up in your hopelessness.

Fantasy: You keep the focus on your dream of how a relationship *could* be rather than on the reality of what you have. You spend a great deal of time pretending your unhealthy situation will miraculously change by fantasizing about the sweetness of your early courtship days.

Which of these 20 characteristics can be identified in the story of the Fab Five? How many of these unhealthy behaviors have you practiced during your dating life or recognized in others? Often only one is enough to damage or end a relationship, and a combination of these characteristics denotes a more complex personality problem. As these unhealthy behaviors continue, your likelihood of being wounded and permanently scarred increases.

WOUNDS AND SCARS

Wounds are temporary damage that was either self-inflicted or received unintentionally. They're the emotions or events that broke or damaged your Picker, such as rape, incest, or verbal abuse. Wounds that haven't yet healed or were never treated properly become scars, which serve as a permanent reminder of a painful situation. The condition of a

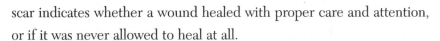

scar indicates whether a wound healed with proper care and attention, or if it was never allowed to heal at all.

We use the acronym **SCARS for Suppressed Conditions Affecting Relationship Success.** SCARS result from an abusive, painful past and/or a dysfunctional childhood. Like physical scars, SCARS provide a certain protection, but in the form of survival skills that we integrate into our personality and bring into our interactions with others. SCARS can be responsible for our attraction to unhealthy people. Some SCARS make victims seek abusers; some trick us into believing that "bad boys/girls must be worth having." Other SCARS make us push people away with beliefs such as "nice guys are so boring."

> 66 **Wounds that haven't yet healed or were never treated properly become scars, which serve as a permanent reminder of a painful situation.** 99

We said earlier that you'll have a hard time attracting those who are healthier than you are; and if you do, they won't stay long. When healthy people identify your excessive needs, they'll quickly reach for the eject button. Healthy people seldom want to play parent, therapist, or punching-bag roles. Below we describe some of the SCARS that trigger your poor picking so you can recognize them and change your unhealthy picking patterns.

SCARS #1: CO-DEPENDENCY

The first SCARS issue we'll examine, co-dependency, has evolved over the last two decades into a convenient generic excuse many people use to explain failed relationships. So what does it mean?

In our generalized definition, we recognize a co-dependent as a person who has been negatively affected by someone else's disease or dysfunction and has learned to adapt by adopting an unhealthy set of behavioral characteristics. This results from participating in extended, unhealthy relationships. Even after the original relationships that created the dysfunction end, individuals continue practicing the behavior on their own or carry it into future relationships.

The predominant "areas of expertise" or most common characteristics found in the co-dependents we've observed are:

◇ control (the balance of power within a relationship is unequal)

◇ manipulation

◇ guilt throwing or accepting of guilt

◇ denial

◇ boundary distortion (an inability to respect another's relationships or privacy)

◇ low self-esteem

◇ confusion of identities

◇ rationalization

◇ minimizing and/or exaggerating

◇ excessive mood swings

◇ addictions

◇ obsessive-compulsive behavior

◇ hyper-vigilance (hyper-awareness, constantly being on the offensive and defensive)

◇ repeated attraction to abusive personalities/relationships

◇ excessive care-taking of others in comparison to oneself

◇ constriction of emotions

❖ stress-related illnesses

❖ inability to express needs or to allow others to meet them

To one degree or another, everyone has some combination of co-dependency characteristics. The co-dependent person, however, exhibits a number of these characteristics to an extremely unhealthy degree. Left untreated, a co-dependent will always be co-dependent. With appropriate treatment through which they can learn to recognize and refrain from harmful behavior, co-dependents can become normal, happy, and functional. Some will require a strong commitment to therapy and self-help types of recovery to overcome their dysfunctional characteristics.

Co-dependents frequently prefer to "fix themselves," which is often what creates their problem in the first place. Let's look at how co-dependent characteristics may prevent you from obtaining or maintaining healthy relationships.

EXERCISE

❧

The Co-Dependency Questionnaire

Dr. Timmen L. Cermak, M.D., developed the following exercise.

Instructions: Answer the 31 questions with a "Yes" or a "No." Middle-of-the-road answers such as "Sometimes" are unacceptable. You have either done it, thought it, felt it, or experienced it—or you haven't. Thus, **only** yes or no answers will provide you with an honest assessment of your condition.

Yes	No	Question
____	____	1. Do you ever worry excessively about any members of your family?
____	____	2. Are you ever embarrassed by another family member's behavior?
____	____	3. Do you feel personally less worthwhile because of another family member's behavior?
____	____	4. Are you often a perfectionist when it comes to things that involve you?
____	____	5. Have you tried to control family members?
____	____	6. Do you take pride in your own self-control?
____	____	7. Do you feel personally inadequate?
____	____	8. Do you feel guilty or responsible for someone else's behavior?
____	____	9. Have you taken over family responsibilities, which you do not believe should be yours?
____	____	10. Have you ever lied to cover up someone else's misbehavior?
____	____	11. Do you often meet other people's needs while you neglect your own?
____	____	12. Do you lack self-confidence in intimate situations?
____	____	13. Are you afraid of being left (alone, abandoned, dumped)?
____	____	14. Are you often unaware of what you are feeling?
____	____	15. Does it feel like you start to get smothered or overwhelmed by people close to you?
____	____	16. Do you tend to see things as either black or white?

Yes	No	Question
____	____	17. Do your emotions ride a roller coaster, with quick ups and downs?
____	____	18. Do you feel complete only when you are in a relationship, or lose your identity in relationships?
____	____	19. Do you often rescue or punish other people?
____	____	20. Are you afraid to let your feelings come out freely?
____	____	21. Do you have dramatic emotional outbursts?
____	____	22. Are you often depressed?
____	____	23. Have you been suicidal?
____	____	24. Is it hard to let down your guard without feeling that a catastrophe might happen?
____	____	25. Do you have compulsions? (Examples: eating, TV, work, sex)
____	____	26. Do you often feel anxious?
____	____	27. Have you tried to ignore problems, hoping they will get better on their own?
____	____	28. Have you been a victim of physical or sexual abuse as an adult?
____	____	29. Do you suffer from stress related medical illnesses?
____	____	30. Are you chemically dependent?
____	____	31. Have you been in a committed relationship with someone who has been actively chemically dependent for two years without seeking outside support?
____	____	**Totals**

Scoring the Co-Dependency Questionnaire

The co-dependency exercise score sheet below contains a list of traits divided into five criterion groups. In parentheses next to each trait is a number that corresponds to the number of the question you answered in the co-dependency questionnaire. If you answered "Yes" to the question, check the trait with the corresponding number. For example, if you checked "Yes" for question 1, the corresponding trait is Worry (1) so you would put a check in the blank in front of "Worry." Continue until you've put a check in front of each trait that corresponds to a question you answered with a "Yes." Some traits have two numbers next to them, indicating they are addressed by more than one question, thus may end up with two checks. For example, if you answer "Yes" to both questions 3 and 7, Personal Inadequacy (3,7) would have two checks. Please note that under Criterion #3 (patterns of unstable and intense relationships) and #4 (loyalty to, or repeated relationships with, personality disorders, substance abuse, or impulse disorders during relationship history), being honest with yourself is imperative. These questions are normally used by a therapist in conjunction with a more thorough relationship history.

Co-Dependency Exercise Score Sheet

Criterion #1

Which willpower traits were demonstrated?

_____ Worry (1)

_____ Embarrassment and shame (2)

_____ Personal inadequacy (3) (7)

_____ Perfectionism (4)

_____ Efforts to control others (5)

_____ Pride in self-control (6)

_____ Guilt and responsibility (8)

Criterion #2

Which dependent/counter-dependent traits are demonstrated?

_____ Taking over responsibility (9)

_____ Covering up (needs others to look okay) (10)

_____ Neglecting own needs (11)

_____ Lack of self-confidence (12)

_____ Fear of being abandoned (13)

Criterion #3

Which borderline traits are demonstrated?

_____ Patterns of unstable and intense relationships (review your personal history or your relationship patterns)

_____ Often unaware of feelings (14)

_____ Feels smothered or overwhelmed by others (15)

_____ Black-and-white thinking (16)

_____ Wide swings in emotion (17)

_____ Enmeshment of identity in relationships (18)

_____ Thoughts of suicide (23)

Criterion #4

Which interpersonal compulsions are demonstrated?

_____ Loyalty to, or repeated relationships with, personality disorders, substance abuse, or impulse disorders from relationship history

_____ Rescuing and punishing (19)

Criterion #5

Which of the following associated symptoms are demonstrated?

_____ Constriction of emotion (20) +/- outbursts (21)

_____ Depression (22)

_____ Hyper-vigilance (24)

_____ Compulsions (25)

_____ Anxiety (26)

_____ Denial (27)

_____ Substance abuse (30)

_____ Recurrent victim of physical/sexual abuse (28)

_____ Stress-related medical illness (29)

_____ Two years without seeking help (31)

Developed by:

Timmen L. Cermak, M.D.

Genesis

1926 Divisadero

San Francisco, CA 94115

Let's examine what your score indicates.

If you checked three items (or only one item in Criterion #4) in three or more separate criterion areas, your score indicates a serious problem with co-dependency, as well as strong attributes of Post Traumatic Stress Disorder (PTSD), as explained in chapter 2. Each characteristic that you have marked with a "Yes" represents an area or aspect of your personality that specifically needs to be addressed if you are to resolve that issue. Co-dependents lie to justify staying in a relationship. Their self-esteem is so low that fear, judgment, insecurity, and failure become more comfortable than losing the relationship. Once those survival traits become habit, co-dependents will treat healthy people as they treated unhealthy ones they were with previously. While these traits offer a defense with an unhealthy partner, they have the opposite effect with a healthy one. For example, using manipulation, control, and hysterics (which worked to control an unstable situation) would destabilize a healthy one.

Unfortunately, the scars and wounds of unhealthy behavior are frequently rooted in our upbringing, which brings us to our second SCARS: Disruptive Lineal Modeling.

SCARS #2: DISRUPTIVE LINEAL MODELING

This SCARS covers:

◇ adult children of alcoholics

◇ blended families

◇ multiple divorces

◇ families suffering the consequences of various addictions (including but not limited to infidelity, gambling, sex, compulsive spending, alcoholism, and eating disorders)

◇ long-term convalescent care

◇ unwanted pregnancy

◇ severe handicaps of a psychological or physical nature that create significant stress for the family (such as multiple sclerosis, cerebral palsy, or depression)

Remember the old cliché, "You are what you eat"? A similar statement can be made about relationships: "You are what you've experienced." If you've been exposed to disruptive behavior from early childhood (see Early Childhood Developmental Model in chapter 5), you're more likely to be attracted to unhealthy partners. In fact, many conditions found within this SCARS may have been practiced and passed down for generations. If your great-grandmother practiced unhealthy behavior, and both your grandmother and your mom adopted it, there's a high probability that you'll follow suit. If your grandmother cooked a roast in an oval pot, you and your mother may do the same—but not

because roast is better when cooked in an oval rather than rectangular pan. You simply practice what you've been taught and repeat what has been modeled for you.

Because it's important that you're able to determine whether or not unresolved issues from childhood affect your relationships, we present the following exercise to help you identify not only the specifics that tripped you up, but the causes and conditions that may prevent you from dating smarter in the future.

When answering the following questions, please respond with either "Yes" or "No" answers **only**. Answer each question. Keep in mind that "Family Members" applies to your parents, grandparents, stepfamily, or significant family members or individuals to whom you were exposed consistently when growing up.

EXERCISE

Disruptive Lineal Modeling Questionnaire

Yes	No	Question
____	____	1. Did you ever assume responsibilities that were clearly not yours due to a family member's dysfunction?
____	____	2. Did you ever compare your home to a friend's whose appeared more "normal" and imagine or desire that yours could be like theirs?
____	____	3. Did you ever feel the need to physically escape (geographically relocate) to get as far away as possible from the pain you were experiencing at home?

Yes	No	Question
____	____	4. Did you ever hope that your parents would get divorced rather than continue to live in the painful environment resultant of their disruptive behavior?
____	____	5. Did you ever feel that you aggravated or incited a parent or parents into further practicing their dysfunction?
____	____	6. Did you ever find yourself disappointed or hurt because a parent was unable to uphold an obligation due to a compulsion, addiction or dysfunction?
____	____	7. Have you ever taken on the responsibility of guarding, shielding, or distancing a family member from the family member who was unhealthy or abusive?
____	____	8. Did you ever feel as if you were used as a mediator or pawn in fights or arguments between a healthy and unhealthy parent (or even in the case where both parents were unhealthy)?
____	____	9. Looking back, do you carry painful or hurtful animosity toward a parent or your parents for the disruptive lifestyle and painful events they subjected you to?
____	____	10. Were you ever afforded the opportunity to talk to someone who could help resolve the unhealthy issues in your family or have you sought that help since leaving the household you grew up in?

Yes	No	Question
____	____	11. Did you ever hide out or make excuses that allowed you to distance yourself from the problems your parent(s) were causing that you were facing at home?
____	____	12. Have you ever suffered insomnia, hypersomnia, nightmares, or night terrors as the result of a parent or parent's behavior, events or abuse?
____	____	13. Were you ever obsessed, fixated, or excessively worried about a parent's unhealthy behavior or how it affected you, your family, or the people, around you?
____	____	14. Did you ever attempt to intervene or did outside intervention push a parent toward seeking a resolution to their problem?
____	____	15. Was a family member's compulsion, addiction, abuse, or behavior the cause of strife and friction between you and another family member?
____	____	16. Have you ever suffered psychosomatic illness due to a parent's behavior?
____	____	17. Did you ever feel frightened, agitated, intimidated, or feel isolated or depressed due to the inability of a parent to overcome or resolve their unhealthy behavior?
____	____	18. Did a parent or parent's problem escalate into physical intimidation with you or another family member?

Yes	No	Question
___	___	19. Did you ever think that a parent or parents suffered from a significant physical, psychological or psychiatric condition or mental health issue?
___	___	20. Did a parent's behavior prompt you to engage them in an aggressive fashion?
___	___	21. Did your parent's dysfunction and their painful interactions negatively affect you without their awareness?
___	___	22. Did you find yourself hopelessly fantasizing that a parent's dysfunction, compulsion, or addiction would miraculously clear up on its own and not exist at all?
___	___	23. Did you ever find yourself ashamed as you bore the burden for your parent's behaviors, actions, or dysfunctions?
___	___	24. Did a parent's dysfunction leave you with the feeling that you were unworthy, unable or undeserving of their love?
___	___	25. Have you ever assumed the burden or responsibility for a parent's unhealthy behavior or dysfunction that you actually had nothing to do with?
___	___	26. Did you ever think that one of your parent's behavior was so dysfunctional, damaging, or disruptive that they warranted being labeled "addictive, abusive, compulsive, or mentally ill?"
___	___	27. Did you ever avoid healthy external contact and interaction with others, essentially withdrawing

Yes	No	Question
		from life itself, because of the association or connection with your parent's dysfunction?
___	___	28. Did you ever undertake an aggressive action to avoid a parent's behavior from being visible or discovered?
___	___	29. Did you ever experience a difficult divorce or were you exposed to multiple marriages as the result of a parent's unhealthy, addictive, abusive, or compulsive behavior?
___	___	30. Did a family member's problem or dysfunction progress to the point where you worried that it terminally affect their physical being and could possibly leave you without a parent at all?
___	___	31. Have you or any family member ever had an eating disorder?
___	___	32. Have you or any family member ever been subjected to profound physical, sexual, or psychological abuse?
___	___	33. Have you or any family member ever suffered long-term chronic illness or intensive long-term care?
___	___	34. During your childhood, did you experience a catastrophic loss of home, life, or property?
___	___	35. Do you relate a personal dysfunction, addiction, or difficulty dating to your childhood experiences or upbrining?
___	___	**Totals**

Disruptive Lineal Modeling Questionnaire Scoring

1 to 8 "Yes" responses (excluding numbers 30 to 35): Chances are you may have grown up with a minor or short-term dysfunction. It has either been resolved through counseling or self-help, or was brief enough that it didn't have lasting effects.

9 to 15 "Yes" responses (excluding numbers 30 to 35): Your character was definitively altered enough to cause problems in your intimate relationships. Your learned habits and behavior probably interfered with your relationships. It's likely that you're either unaware of the level of dysfunction you inherited and its affect on your social life, or you spend excess time blaming others for your present relationship woes.

16 to 29 "Yes" responses (excluding numbers 30 to 35): You were profoundly affected by events of your upbringing. We hope you've consciously addressed these issues with a therapist who specializes in your specific problems. We also encourage you to participate in a support group. The sharing of experiences with others who have similar issues and were able to resolve them can help you overcome your own.

30 or more "Yes" responses (including any numbered 30 through 35): Two things are likely: First, it will be nearly impossible for you to attain and maintain a quality relationship with a healthy person without getting help. If your issues aren't addressed, they will inevitably lead you to a revolving door of relationship failures. Second, you're almost assured to attract someone or be attracted to someone as unhealthy as you are. It's possible you've become immune to your unhealthy behavior. Denial can prevent you from making changes necessary to succeed in relationships. Your unhealthy ways can become so much a part of you that you don't recognize what's wrong.

One special note: 29 "Yes" answers and a "Yes" to any question numbered from 30 to 35 indicates severe denial of your problem and the consequences of growing up in an unhealthy environment. It also indicates that you should seek professional help immediately.

In the first two SCARS (co-dependency and unhealthy lineal modeling) we examined issues that are more family-based and internal from cause to effect. The third SCARS examines wounds of an external nature

SCARS #3: POST-TRAUMATIC PERSONALITY IMPRINT (PTPI)

A **Post-Traumatic Personality Imprint (PTPI)** is a combination of character flaws resulting from negative circumstances that alters your personality so drastically that it adversely affects your dating life.

People who've been abused learn reactions and responses to survive experiences they've suffered. As a result, their behavior intuitively responds to certain stimuli. They either attract more calamities through bad decisions or they sabotage healthy situations to confirm their insecurity. They have a tough time reaching out to give or receive. Their damaged ego can never be satisfied.

The Confirmation Syndrome

Egomaniacs think the world revolves around them. Those with inferiority complexes believe they're completely unworthy of anything. Yet both types have the same basic problem—they think *only* of themselves. Driven by fear, they need constant validation. Individuals that suffer PTPI exhibit ego-driven characteristics that we call the **Confirmation Syndrome.**

The Confirmation Syndrome comes from insecurity, the need for constant validation that everything is okay and that you have worth. You need to hear or say "I love you" regularly. Many of your sentences end with a version of "Do you know what I mean?" You make numerous calls just to ask, "What are you up to?" Or you're constantly aware of another person's schedule, movements, and contacts. These techniques create a false sense of security. Your need for approval can turn to extreme disapproval for friends and associates who don't buy into your way. When the Confirmation Syndrome reaches an unhealthy peak, what we call a **ParaSnooper** mentality becomes evident.

ParaSnoopers are people who selectively investigate other people's personal belongings, including their drawers, appointment and address books, wallets, purses, and mail in a desperate, paranoid attempt to uncover evidence to confirm what they already believe. These people have been scarred and become hyper-vigilant. In some cases, their fears are warranted due their bad picks. However, if they act out these fears with healthy people (picks), ParaSnoopers will break their partners' trust, breach their privacy, and drive them away.

Much of this behavior mimics **Attachment Disorder, Separation Anxiety,** and **Obsessive-Compulsive Disorder,** three forms of anxiety disorder in which the sufferer assumes an overwhelming feeling that abandonment is inevitable. Here are examples of each so you can see how they differ:

◇ **Attachment Disorder**
This condition urges you to put up so many walls that getting close or attaining intimacy is nearly impossible. You may have experienced infidelity in marriage and have an overwhelming fear that everyone will cheat on you. To the opposite extreme, you may cling so tightly to another person that they feel they are incapable of escaping your suffocating grasp.

◇ Separation Anxiety

This condition is more obsessive-compulsive by nature. You may have hysterical outbreaks and fits of crying, make threats against yourself or others, and develop a consuming fear that your partner will abandon the relationship—even if he or she is only going to get the mail. Your lack of trust, extreme jealousy, and salvation mentality (intense crisis-driven rescuing or counter-dependence) is evident. This "salvation mentality" shows in statements such as, "I'll die if you leave." "Who'll feed the dog if you leave?" "Who'll fix the car when it breaks down?" Your commitment is dictated by how much responsibility you can get them to take.

◇ Obsessive-Compulsive Disorder

The fear behind this condition makes you smothering. You're so desperate to "make this one work" that you quickly overload and burn out your partner. You may go overboard when giving gifts, flowers, cards, and compliments. You have a constant need for physical exposure with your partner, whether for sex or just being in his or her presence. Even short bus trips or time you partner spends with friends or relatives can become unbearable. Your love interest is your *only* interest—24 hours a day, seven days a week.

❝ You may find yourself bitter and despondent if you're judged for your disabilities rather than appreciated for your abilities. ❞

Where's the off switch? Obsessive-compulsive people often need contact long after the relationship is over, and may ultimately get charged with stalking or phone harassment. They play the relationship over and over in their minds, comparing each potential date and relationship to a past one, but no one measures up.

People with these conditions have excessive baggage. Some of this baggage begins with a painful event: the original scar. If the original issues don't heal, the behavior becomes more pronounced over time. This can make maintaining a long-term friendship nearly impossible and an intimate long-term relationship becomes even harder. You may find yourself bitter and despondent if you're judged for your disabilities rather than appreciated for your abilities.

SCARS #4: SITUATIONAL SABOTAGE

In SCARS #4, individuals operate from two bases. A person with the first tendency, self-destruction through control, makes both subtle and obvious efforts to control a relationship, which eventually leads to confrontation, rejection, and failure. The second basis is intentional compromise and deceptive attraction. Intentional compromise exists when you choose a negative path by rationalizing that the positives will outweigh the negatives. "I'm choosing money over love." Deceptive attraction exists when someone who's inexperienced in relationships becomes gullible, easily overwhelmed, or impressed. The deceiver feeds off a weaker person's desire to be loved or feel important. They use and abuse people for their own gain, with no remorse or intention of a long-term commitment. We're going to examine several of the most common types of Situational Sabotage.

Control Freaks

What is control and why do we attempt to control others? Control comes from fear, which can develop from a lack of faith. Let's examine two primary fears: the fear of not getting what we want and the fear of losing something we already have. Fear drives us to control people and situations at all cost to get what we want. Insecurity and low self-esteem,

combined with spiritual malnutrition, push us to extremes for getting our desired results. There's little belief that everything will be okay and no confidence to let things evolve naturally. When fear gets to us, we try turning the process of love into a predictable event to feel safer.

Common examples of control freak types are:

◇ The work-out fanatic

◇ The shop-a-holic

◇ The neat freak

◇ Mr. or Ms. "my way or the highway"

◇ "I wear the pants in this family"

◇ The used car salesman (aggressive, domineering, loud, untrustworthy)

◇ The religious addict

◇ The sports addict

◇ The "not tonight, dear, I have a headache" (withholds sex to control a relationship)

◇ The swinger's partner (who partakes in sex against his or her own taste or values to keep an eye on or control the partner)

Each can be attractive (in moderation) to a potential partner since they may share a common interest. But in chronic and intense extremes, these characteristics become a foundation for relationship failure.

Financial Insecurity

Some of us choose money over love as fear of not having enough of our own creates financial insecurity. The term "gold digger" applies here. If money worries you, you may make a poor pick and stay in a relationship if the financial benefits outweigh the personal negatives. The effects of this type of situational sabotage are most often seen in women

in their late 30s to early 40s, as their spouses suffer a mid-life crisis. While these women may have been a "trophy" at one time, a real possibility exists that they could wake up one day and find themselves replaced by a much younger version who can be controlled easier and cost less. If this happens, you can end up angry and bitter after giving up a good chunk of your life and career only to lose what you were with him for in the first place—the money.

Baggage

What happens when you or your partner call out someone else's name while in bed? Or that name frequently comes up during intimate conversations? Or a gift isn't appreciated because it brings back memories, or you must avoid a particular place for fear of running into the person? The old term "ball and chain" has new meaning.

Failure to properly close a relationship has initiated many a fight and ended many a budding romance. An individual may

> 66 Failure to properly close a relationship has initiated many a fight and ended many a budding romance. 99

have attempted to close a relationship with an unhealthy person, but may find him- or herself at the mercy of an obsessive-compulsive person and possibly even stalked. It can be frightening when your current love interest has made several attempts to stop your ex, who remains undaunted and relentless.

What if you're the one who's unable to cut ties with your ex? You continue taking calls, answering e-mail, responding to pages, scheduling lunches or other meetings. Because you're emotionally unavailable to fully invest in a relationship with your new love interest, he or she will eventually discover your problem. Two's company; three's a crowd.

Emotional, psychological, physical, or perceived infidelity is the kiss of death for a relationship.

Someone who can't let go of an ex isn't ready for a new relationship. If your partner still has abnormal or unnecessary contact with his or her ex, this is a clear warning sign that you need to bail out quickly. Otherwise, you may be treated as if *you're* the ex. Such a triangular relationship isn't worth the hurt parties typically experience. However, if you're dating someone with children, or have them yourself, contact with a former spouse or love interest to effectively and appropriately rear that child may be necessary.

Office Romance

It's common to spend significantly more time with fellow workers than working on your love life. No wonder office romances develop! A real danger comes from deceptive attraction, especially when you're attracted to a person in a position of power who behaves in a manner consistent with sexual harassment.

Although not all office romances are inappropriate or doomed, they certainly don't have a great track record or reputation. When office romances fail, they can cause disruption when co-workers take sides, pretend it didn't exist, perceive favoritism, experience jealousy, feel a lack of confidentiality, or gossip. Many companies concerned about this problem save employee e-mails and voice-mail records for up to five years. A special set of problems exists if one party is married.

Gunslingers

They ride Harleys. They drive Corvettes, Porsches, BMWs, jet skis, and surfboards. They sport Armani, Tommy Hilfiger, Donna Karan, and more. If what they have is bigger, better, and more expensive, they win. Some have implants, more "carats" than a grocery store, great abdominal muscles, and legs to die for. They're the object of everyone's desire and know it. They're smooth to a science. We're talking about the men and women who are big game hunters, with a trophy room and lots of notches on their gun belt after many emotional slaughters. The trail of broken hearts and leftover baggage resembles a 120-car pile up on the interstate. To them, you're a number—replaceable, erasable, nothing more than a pit stop on the road of one-upmanship and trophy hunting.

Here's the twist. You want them and they couldn't care less. You want them because they *don't* want you. These are the bad boys and girls we fantasize about having. They're tantalizing and exciting. They can have anything or anyone they want and you delude yourself into thinking that you're *The One* even though their last five exes were insignificant to them. You perform like a trained seal in hopes of capturing their heart (if they have one). You want to be the one to break the wild horse no one else could. You convince yourself that because they're a challenge, they must be worth having. You may decide to wait for your chance to become their next ex. Meanwhile, nice guys finish last in your race; they appear too needy, boring,

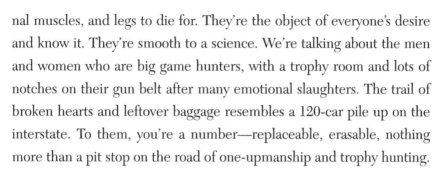

You want them and they couldn't care less. You want them because they *don't* want you.

predictable, and give the impression they'll always be waiting while you date the losers. You sink a nice guy or gal with a single shot: "If I can have you, why on earth would I want you?"

When you stand on a gunslinger's turf, expect to be shot down. After all, they earned the "reputation" gunslinger (player, bad boy, nasty girl— take your pick). Somewhere in the middle is a self-assertive, loving achiever that we'll help you identify in chapter 6 by using the **15-Minute Find.** You don't need to get shot down to learn.

The different types of situational sabotage are endless. However, most saboteurs have an unconscious drive that's relentless in nature. It can annoy a significant other enough to abandon the relationship. Their behavior may be acceptable in moderation or on a cultural plane (such as religion, cooking, working out, and primping, or excessive clothing purchases), but they take it to chronic and intense extremes.

As you have seen above, situational sabotage can cause financial hardship, social alienation, and the loss of relationships with family and friends. In some cases, it can even cause employment failure, bankruptcy or continued subjection to a hopelessly abusive relationship.

Give yourself a huge pat on the back. You've swallowed some hard truths and looked at the causes and conditions that comprised your relationship history to the present. The evaluation you've experienced so far and knowledge you've gained is half the solution to your problems—understanding what your problems are and why they exist. You've laid the groundwork necessary and cleared your heart and mind of "baggage" so that new solutions can become your way of life. The best is yet to come!

While you've taken responsibility for your part in a relationship failure, we feel it remiss to let society off the hook for its involvement. Chapter 5 briefly examines the influence society may have had on the evolution of divorce and the development of the modern-day disposable relationship.

5

It's Not All Your Fault

Remember when you were six years old and you wanted a bright red fire truck (doll, or other gift) so badly for Christmas that you began lobbying for it in August? You couldn't pass a store without pleading for this "dream gift." You studied it like an archaeologist searching for the missing link. When your older brother or sister took you shopping for your parents' gift, you wanted to give them something as special as what they were probably giving you. At age six, you figured the latest set of mega-magic markers and the newest video game were the coolest presents you could give mom and dad. When you bought them (with your parents' money and under your brother's or sister's watchful eye), you were so sure they would love them as much as you did.

On Christmas morning, you breathlessly looked under the tree. There it was—the "dream gift" you had obsessed over for months. You were ecstatic but noticed that Mom and Dad didn't look as happy with their gifts as you were with yours. You quickly put their apparent disappointment behind you and went back to playing with your dream gift. Hours passed like minutes as you reveled in your big score. Three hours later, you finally noticed your other presents and began to open them as well. As days went by, you became more excited by your other toys and less infatuated with your dream gift so you placed it on a shelf. Six months later, your dream gift still collected dust as you played with all your gifts except the one you had wanted most.

Had you built up your dream gift to the point that it could never meet your expectations? When you got what you thought you *wanted*—the gift that represented the ultimate prize—it essentially lost all importance. When you got what you *needed*—gifts that provided the entertainment you desired—you realized they were what you really wanted all along.

Our "needs" and "wants" can become easily confused. We tend to chase "wants," intense desires to obtain something, which are driven by emotion. Such desires are usually more like hunger demanding instant gratification than food for long-term satisfaction. "Needs" are often less exciting and are usually based on logical or intellectual assumptions that they will meet a desired goal. The key to successful relationships is to more closely align our wants with our needs so that the probable outcome will be long-term success rather than short-term gratification.

The story at the beginning of the chapter illustrates three points:

1 **Our motives and desires influence how we strive for what we want.** This is especially evident when we enter relationships. What do *all* men and *all* women *want more* than anything else? **What they cannot have.** When we're told that we cannot have something we desire, we want it all the more. When we're told that someone is unattainable, our desire for the person increases. Strong desire clouds our ability to discern whether a person can meet our *needs* or whether we simply *want* them (quite possibly for all the wrong reasons).

2 **What we give great importance to can easily become disposable and replaceable.** From August through December, the "dream gift" was "it."

Yet, shortly after Christmas, it was put away for safekeeping. Becoming aware of the distinction between wants and needs allows us to re-prioritize "needs" to become "wants." Otherwise, we keep striving for what we think we want and rarely get what we need. When we get what we need, our "wants" are usually satisfied as well. Focusing on getting what you *need* to be happy increases your odds for achieving satisfaction. Failing to address the needs that will make you happy may result in your substituting one quick fix or short-lived thrill after another but rarely will lead to long-term joy.

3 **Good intentions don't always bring the satisfaction intended.** The parents, by failing to remember what it was like to be six and not showing appreciation for their child's idea of the "perfect gift" for them, illustrate this point. Their apparent lack of interest in the gifts taught the child that what's "important" to one person can be meaningless to another. Still, the parents should have responded to the well-intended gifts with enthusiasm and excitement to boost confidence, fulfill his/her expectations, and make him/her feel appreciated. Seemingly benign situations like this can set the stage for the next generation of divorces.

As adults, we see that expectations can vary between partners in a relationship. If we can't communicate to one another what we *need,* we may find ourselves trying to satisfy the wrong needs. Or we may scrap a relationship because we haven't learned to align our expectations with the work our partner must do to fulfill our wants and needs. The child's story illustrates how even six-year-olds engage in unfulfilling and unappreciated relationships. Our heritage and ineffective teachers and models reinforce our tendency to get caught up in passion and turn our backs on the logical processes required to be successful in relationships.

Early Childhood Developmental Model

We encourage you to explore and deal with any childhood issues that influence the success of your relationships. We want to share with you a Developmental Model (created by an instructor at the Johnson Institute in Minneapolis, Minnesota). Although there are dozens of early childhood developmental models, we want to relate early childhood parenting to behavior learned that would be practiced later in life. It will become obvious as you read through this model how people learn to attract or be attracted to the wrong person time and again. In this model, we'll equate a mother's love with that of an emotional gas pump.

Birth to Three Years

Between the ages of birth to nine months, children react purely out of instinct. They sleep when they're tired, and cry when they're hungry, tired, or need to be changed. They have no sense of right or wrong and fail to get punch lines of good jokes.

Between the ages of nine months and three years children learn to crawl, walk, talk, and explore their world and environment. Exploration may include putting things they shouldn't into their mouth, skinning their knees, toilet training, and recognizing boundaries and discipline, to name just a few.

During this time of exploring and experiencing both pain and pleasure, it's critical that parents be available to reinforce, affirm, discipline, and provide information. Through interaction with one or both parents, children's personalities develop. As they grow and experience both positive and negative aspects of life, they'll return to their parents for reinforcement as needed. Parents are much like emotional gas pumps to whom children can go when they need love, understanding, compassion, or information. At such times, the pump needs to be on. At other times, the pump needs to be turned off to encourage independence, exploration, and learning.

The four scenarios below illustrate the effects a single mother's support, or lack thereof, has on her child's development. Each example illustrates possible personality traits that may develop from direct parental action or inaction.

> 66 Parents are much like emotional gas pumps to whom children can go when they need love, understanding, compassion, or information. 99

Scenario One: Emotional Pump Is Completely Off

This mother either doesn't care, or is too incapacitated to care. The child skins his knee, hurts himself, or wants recognition for something he did well, but Mom's pump is off so she provides nothing. She forgets to pack his lunch or pick him up at daycare. This child learns that "no one cares" so he takes what he wants without regard for the consequences or feelings of others. Without experiencing compassion, sympathy, or empathy, this child develops none of these qualities himself. He may develop psychotic tendencies (the inability to have empathy or sympathy for others). He wants what he wants and doesn't care how he gets it.

Scenario Two: Emotional Pump Is Turned On Excessively

This type of mother has the Boston Strangler grip on her child. He's never allowed out of her sight and is meticulously guarded, groomed, manicured, and "dressed to the nines." This mother frequently isolates her child from other children, saying, "They're not good enough for you to play with." She's obsessive, possessive, and compulsive. Other children play team sports, games, and jump rope. Her child, whom she's convinced is a "prodigy," spends most free time practicing endlessly to develop a talent that's not there. This child is a symbol—a mirror image of her perfection. He has every need met before he can express or ask. This child lacks social skills and is consumed with perfection; his first and only love will be himself. This is how the narcissistic personality is formed.

Scenario Three: Emotional Pump Is Off When It Should Be On and On When It Should Be Off

When this child turns to the emotional pump for reinforcement after exploring his world, the pump is off. Mom's unhealthy relationship, an addiction, or another distraction makes her unavailable to provide the attention a child needs. When she's in better spirits, she tries offsetting the effects of earlier neglect by overcompensating with excessive attention. She may buy exorbitant gifts and toys, coddle, or reward the child in an attempt to bribe him to forget her earlier behavior. As the child grows, he learns it's his mother who needs parenting when she's incapacitated and learns to use guilt and manipulation when he doesn't get what he wants. In later years, these children may raise the younger children in their family, assume household responsibilities, and consequently forfeit much of their childhood. This most commonly occurs in families where an addiction, eating disorder, or abusive relationship exists. Children in this type of environment develop strong co-dependent characteristics and frequently play roles such as the Family Hero, the Scapegoat, the Lost Child, or the Mascot (See sidebar, p. 118.)

A family can have more than one person playing the same role or one person playing more than one role during the course of their childhood or adult lives. Gender and age differences can also affect which roles they take on.

Above all, the children in scenario number three learned to survive by following three basic rules:

◇ Don't talk

◇ Don't trust

◇ Don't feel

These children learned when growing up not to talk about their family's dysfunction. They developed distrust of the parent with an inconsistent gas pump and became accustomed to living with inconsistency, failure, and chaos. They learned to suppress feelings and lower their expectations in relationships so that the intolerable became tolerable (from Claudia Black's *It Will Never Happen to Me*).

Because these children grew up with dysfunction as their norm, they will invariably attract what was modeled for them when selecting relationships. The person they pick will mirror the basic rules of don't talk, trust, or feel because they know how to get along with and will be attracted to such people. If you don't trust one another, you operate from a mode of independence and you don't have to rely on others. If both you and your partner have spent a lifetime not feeling, you not only ignore the feelings and avoid the consequences when problems are present in your relationship, but are unlikely to take responsibility for resolving them or even to talk them out.

As a result of operating out of these rules learned in early childhood, an unhealthy couple can suffer in silence for years—even indefinitely—without working out their problems or resolving issues. No matter how frustrated this dysfunctional pair gets with each other, they simply don't

1. **The Family Hero:** This is usually, but not always, the firstborn. An overly responsible perfectionist, this child tries to take the focus off parental dysfunction by achieving positively inside and outside the home. His or her primary goal is to deflect attention from the unhealthy parents with positive actions such as academic excellence, athletic achievement, and assuming parental responsibilities. Such children take over so that no one will notice their family's problems and act as a parental substitute.

2. **The Scapegoat:** This is often the second-born child. Such children are starved for attention, as they can't compete with the older sibling or the parent's dysfunction. So they get attention through negative behavior such as theft, drug or alcohol usage, or association with disruptive individuals. They deflect attention from the family or unhealthy parent with negative behavior.

3. **The Lost Child:** This child is probably the most adversely affected and is usually third in the birth order. Because one sibling is receiving attention through positive behavior, and the other through negative behavior, The Lost Child is frequently ignored or forgotten. Unable to com-

pete with the chaos, he or she withdraws from the family and society. Isolation prevents Lost Children from developing interaction skills so they often develop imaginary friends, hide in their rooms, or escape into music, art, computers, or video games. As adults, these children tend to end up in solitary jobs such as accounting, architecture, and the arts—careers requiring minimal interaction with others. They're shy, introverted, and inclined to suffer from eating disorders and psychosomatic illnesses such as migraines, ulcers, and high blood pressure. Failure to complete childhood issues makes them attracted to unhealthy, addictive, and disruptive individuals, the only types of relationships they know.

4. **The Mascot:** They are usually fourth-born or the baby of the family. In an effort to correct the mistakes made with the Lost Child and Scapegoat, the parents and the Family Hero usually try harder to give the Mascot attention. The Mascot's forte is humor, used to deflect attention from the family. They're daring, animated, comical, and rely on extreme behavior, bordering on unacceptable. They are the classic court jesters.

feel or talk, and thus let the frustration go on for years. Individuals who operate in one of these roles commonly will close a relationship with another co-dependent or adult child, only to pick yet another addict/alcoholic or adult child of dysfunction. Despite their recent misery, they are comfortable with what's familiar.

> **66** As a result of operating out of these rules learned in early childhood, an unhealthy couple can suffer in silence for years—even indefinitely—without working out their problems or resolving issues. **99**

Scenario Four:
Pump's On When It's Supposed to Be On, Off When It's Supposed to Be Off

The child in this scenario explores and gets emotional validation, physical affection, and psychological reinforcement when he needs it. The parent is capable of providing consistent discipline, setting boundaries, and giving attention. Interaction is spontaneous, joyful, and healthy, as is interaction with friends and family. Since the family is healthy, their friends and relatives tend to be healthy too.

AGE THREE TO AGE TWELVE

What children learn between the ages of nine months to three years, they'll practice between the ages of three and twelve. Survival skills get honed as they get older and expand their activities. A child with psychotic tendencies may torture small animals, get into many fights, lie, and steal. They take and do what they want with no regard for consequences or effects on others. Co-dependents or adult children of alco-holics/addicts continue practicing one of their roles to a greater degree. The narcissistic personality becomes more withdrawn/introverted as the parent projects their perfectionist desires onto social or scholastic are-nas. The normal child continues developing normally, participating in social activities and sports, playing with friends, and so on.

AGE TWELVE TO AGE FOURTEEN

What happens between the ages of twelve and fourteen? Puberty! Children experience sleepovers and summer camps, which provide opportunities for bonding with the same sex away from home. If chil-dren from unhealthy home environments can spend significant time with someone of the same gender and age in a healthy environment, they might adopt some of the healthy child's characteristics. Being exposed to healthy modeling can sufficiently turn their negatively affected personality to-ward something more normal. Certain environmental conditions must be present for this to happen, but the influence of a same-sex best friend and healthy modeling can reshape a good portion of their personality.

> **66** What children learn between the ages of nine months to three years, they'll practice between the ages of three and twelve. **99**

AGE FOURTEEN TO AGE EIGHTEEN

We've said throughout the book that you can only practice the pro-gramming you know. If you had no healthy best-friend model from twelve to fourteen, you'll continue to practice what you practiced from ages three to twelve. If you had enough healthy contact to make a major change, you'll practice your newly established behavior from fourteen to eighteen.

AGE EIGHTEEN TO AGE TWENTY-ONE

What happens between ages eighteen and twenty-one? Independent living sets in. People move out, attend college, get jobs, get married. Once again a unique opportunity presents itself. Those who go to college or into the service most likely have roommates who provide opportunity for same-age and same-gender bonding. As before, this bonding must be with a healthy individual or individuals. The primary difference is that as young adults, the presence of healthy parents and modeling is not necessary. An age and gender role model can probably show you what a normal, healthy relationship is.

> 66 Most importantly, we want you to know that if you can see it and understand it, you're halfway to changing it. 99

Alice Cooper said it best in a song: "I'm 18, I'm not a boy, I'm not a man. I'm stuck in the middle without any plan." This is a door that opens for the last time before permanent adult personality characteristics develop. If all conditions for healthy modeling are met, it's possible to adopt another person's behavior and develop more normal relationships in the future. However, you may have missed this last chance for free mental health, so you'll again continue practicing what you have learned before.

Age Twenty-One and Beyond

If your behavior is unhealthy and you're over age twenty-one, this book offers the tools for making the changes you desire. Chances are you'll be spending time with a therapist or in a self-help group to gain information and attain validation.

We provided this developmental model to help you relate to the origins of a dysfunctional childhood (unhealthy lineal modeling) so that if you did have one, you'll have a concrete understanding of the roots of your behavior and poor decision making. Most importantly, we want you to know that if you can see it and understand it, you're halfway to changing it.

'Til Death Do Us Part?

The human race is growing biologically, genetically, and medically at a rate dramatically faster than evolution ever intended. The proof is in history books, which show that the average life expectancy just 400 years ago was between 30 and 35 years of age. In those days, women became "old enough" for childbearing at the age of 14 or 15 and either quickly marched to the altar or were assigned "old maid" status by the age of 17 or 18. Pregnancy within the first year or two of marriage was not only common but expected. Even if a woman survived childbirth, diseases, and difficult living conditions, she rarely lived long enough to observe the birth of her first grandchild.

In the last 400 years, due to advances in science and other factors, our average life expectancy has more than doubled to around 75 years. In the previous 10,000 years, life expectancy did not increase significantly. In the past, children probably witnessed a relationship between their biological parents for 10 to 14 years, even if both parents survived to their life expectancy of age 30 to 35 (which was rare). However, our concept of longevity in relationships has not grown accordingly.

Two major factors contribute to our inability to attain and maintain healthy long-term relationships. One is the lack of realistic modeling of successful long-term relationships growing at the same rate as our age expectancy. How many 30-, 40-, or 50-year marriages are you aware of? How many examples of *happy, healthy, long-term* (more than 20-year) commitments or interactions have you seen? How many of these included children who successfully followed their parents' footsteps? Do you know people who are on their second, third, or fourth marriages and have no idea why the first, second, or third ended? Four hundred years ago, staying together "'til death do us part" was typical. Now, because our life expectancy has increased but our knowledge of what makes a relationship strong and healthy hasn't kept pace, staying together for life (which can amount to 50 years or more!) is far more difficult.

The second major factor contributing to our inability to attain and maintain healthy long-term relationships—the evolution of disposable relationships—is derived from cultural influences and our intolerance for pain. When we combine this with an insatiable desire for instant gratification, we have the recipe for getting into and out of relationships in record time. It's important to understand that this problem is not only about our inability to bring closure. Tracing its roots even further reveals a widespread inability to grieve as an individual, family, nation, and world. We don't know how to grieve or close relationships, and will do just about anything to avoid doing either.

BIG BOYS DON'T CRY

Grief is one of the least discussed topics in America. We learn early on to deny our emotional and spiritual sides in relation to bad feelings.

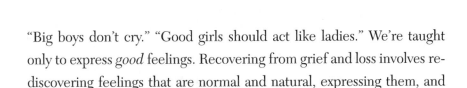

"Big boys don't cry." "Good girls should act like ladies." We're taught only to express *good* feelings. Recovering from grief and loss involves rediscovering feelings that are normal and natural, expressing them, and reviewing the process of successfully closing relationships.

Consider a child whose pet gets run over by a car. Rather than discussing and resolving the loss of that pet with the child, a normal reaction is to avoid the issue by telling the child, "It's okay, honey, we'll get you another dog right away." As the child becomes an adult, he or she tends to assume that all loses will be miraculously handled in the same manner.

Do you remember your first boy- or girlfriend, your first puppy love? You "knew" the person was the one for you. Two weeks later, your "crush" was running around the playground with someone new. You cried for five days and vowed never to eat or come out of your room again. To ease your pain, your parents proclaimed "there are plenty of fish in the sea," reinforcing the "replace it rather than resolve it" attitude. You learned to seek out instant gratification and relief instead of discussing your loss and resolving your pain.

As adults, we translate this to: "If things don't work out in this relationship, I'll simply replace him (or her) with someone else." Failure to close relationships properly creates a revolving door through which scenarios repeat time and again.

Each generation that fails to learn how to properly close relationships can only pass on what is familiar to them.

CLOSE THE DOOR BEHIND YOU

Much like a death is the end of a life, a divorce is the end of a relationship. Inadequate closure in a divorce or long-term relationship can lead to disruption and poor relationships in the future. To successfully close a relationship, you must grieve. This involves reviewing it and allowing your emotional and spiritual feelings to evolve. Then you can complete the relationship and move on. Only expressing and hearing the truth and taking responsibility for our own accountability will close a relationship. Rather than accepting the responsibility necessary and freeing ourselves, we often fall back on the excuse that "others are to blame" and avoid the real issues we need to face.

Divorcing parents unwittingly prepare their children to take their places in line as the next generation of divorcing adults. *Prenuptial agreements have become the standard for planned failure.* When a couple prepares a prenuptial agreement, they are essentially declaring that "there's a better than average chance that this relationship will fail. That being true, what's mine now (and maybe even some of yours) will be mine later."

> 66 Divorcing parents unwittingly prepare their children to take their places in line as the next generation of divorcing adults. 99

Many people believe that only a person who has experienced a similar loss can understand that type of loss. Society, however, frequently encourages us to express mild pacification through ridiculous comments such as: "I understand what you're going through." "We've all been there." "You'll get over it." "If you don't think about it, it won't hurt as much." Such abstract identification fails to recognize the unique and individual nature that makes a relationship valuable and important. Learn to forgive people for their ignorance of your particular situation and don't expect them to meet your needs, as society has badly equipped and misinformed us about dealing with closure and recovery from grief.

It is imperative that you do your best to properly close a relationship, or you may continue to remain stuck in a cycle of frustration and repetition. How many bad relationships must you have before you realize that you're not getting appropriate closure? Continuing to deny loss will perpetuate your tendency to move on and engage again in unhealthy relationships.

DISPOSABLE MARRIAGES

We've taken you through your history and your childhood. We've taught you what to look for in relation to inappropriate closure. Now we want to show you the numbers, facts, and sad truth about the cultural and systemic evolution of divorce in America. In 1991, studies conducted in the United States by the Rand Corporation indicated that 54.8% of all new marriages in 1990 ended in divorce within one year. Over 50% of those married in our country spent a fortune on weddings; invited family and friends; made intricate arrangements for the "big day"; stood in front of their family, friends, and God; declared their love for one another; and proclaimed, "I do, until death do us part." Within just 365 days, their next announcement was "I did. I wish I hadn't and now I want out."

What circumstances led to the disintegration of their vows of commitment in less than one year? Some possible explanations we've heard include:

⬦ "He couldn't understand why she persisted in taking her makeup off with the white towels instead of cotton balls. He said nothing because he loved her."

⬦ "Was he lazy, or just dense? Why couldn't he put dishes in the dishwasher that was only 12 inches away, and when he did bother to try, why couldn't he stack them correctly?"

◇ "Why couldn't he put his underwear in the laundry basket instead of on the chair, floor, or closet doorknob?"

◇ "He wanted a stinky, smelly dog. I wanted a sweet little kitten."

◇ "She wanted a stupid cat. I wanted a playful loving dog."

◇ "Cold didn't just refer to the climate she created in our bedroom."

◇ "She felt that she wore the pants in the family because she made the most money."

Little surprises, also called reality, tend to arise shortly after the honeymoon is over. There are a million and one questions that are rarely asked or answered before people say "I do." In this day of the disposable marriage, the commitment to "love, honor, cherish, and obey until death do us part" frequently results in tragic, disruptive, and sometimes even fatal consequences. Often couples make little or no investment spiritually, emotionally, or psychologically *before* taking vows. They may desire to commit to a long-term relationship, but a large number are incapable of sustaining the commitment for even a year, let alone a lifetime.

Individuals who participated in the 1990–1991 Divorce Study were followed for a year after their divorce. Despite their desire to maintain a healthy relationship, many simply didn't have the skills needed to be successful. Seventy percent of those who got divorced remarried within one year. They may have been so desperate for companionship that they didn't allow adequate time for closure and for resolving the issues that caused the demise of their first marriage. They didn't resolve the key issues that caused their marriage to disintegrate or allow enough time to heal them. Instead, they married again, in haste, for unhealthy reasons. They simply replaced one person with another. Coincidentally, of the 70% who remarried, approximately 36% divorced again. While their odds seem to be improving, nearly four out of every ten marriages failed a second time.

Why does this happen? Disposable relationships, multiple partners, sex addiction, relationship addiction, and every other form of sabotage known to relationships is modeled for us 24 hours a day by television shows, soap operas, dramatizations, real life stories, the tabloids, and the Internet. This pervasive reinforcement of unhealthy relationships combined with the biological, genetic, and cultural quantum leap in life expectancy noted earlier minimizes our chance for a healthy relationship. It sets up the perfect scenario for relationship failure and for continually "picking" poor relationships. Individuals who carry unresolved, unclosed relationships into their next one further complicate the problem. They end up with so many skeletons in their closet that it's no wonder communication breakdowns and commitment failures become a consistent pattern.

What makes us jump from relationship to relationship? What drives people to seek the quick fix? A perfect example is the hysteria that surrounded the movie *Titanic* and its leading character portrayed by actor Leonardo DiCaprio. What drove the girls wild over Leo? What made them go back and watch the movie four, five, even six times or buy up the books and magazines that featured him on their cover? What did he have that they wanted so much?

> 66 **Individuals who carry unresolved, unclosed relationships into their next one further complicate the problem.** 99

Leo wasn't as incredible as attendance numbers indicated. This heartthrob inspired a love fantasy in a very specific audience. Girls ages 12 to 18 dramatically led the stampede to see him. Could it have been that this group identified with the girl in *Titanic*, who was repressed, controlled by her mother, and the victim of a predetermined destiny? Perhaps it was also fascination with the idea of an exciting, spontaneous, and unpredictable love interest materializing as the ultimate escape plan. Being swept away in romance appeared a sexy alternative for a life full of compromise and mediocrity to appease one's parents.

We can't deny that the movie was full of excitement and suspense—all the things young love is made of. But like the ship "Titanic," young love rarely goes the distance. It's based on feelings, emotions, and rapidly changing personalities that have few, if any, healthy traits or interests in common. The particular brand of romantic love that drove this movie and its characters seems a common thread in our culture. We love an underdog and there's nothing like an apparent lost cause. The movie's plot resembles an all-too-familiar problem that we call "chasing a heart that's unavailable." When we get what we've *wanted*, we find it doesn't want us in return; it's not practical, feasible, or what we *needed* all along.

Living in the moment can feel great—for the moment. But throwing our young impulsive selves to the wind and shouting that life is "ours for the taking" lacks the plan or practical application to make it work. When we're dealing with love we're dealing with feelings, which are thoughts rather than facts. When we change thoughts, the feelings change with them and the outcome does as well. Thus the desired happy ending can change in a nanosecond. The Titanic sailed on its reputation of greatness, but the iceberg proved how quickly it could sink. The same is true in love, as so many of us have learned too well.

 # HEALTHY ENDINGS

Through direct interaction with individuals whose relationships were in complete disarray, we've found that in a majority of instances, the relationships were damaged to the point that saving them was an unlikely, unrealistic option. The love was gone, as was the caring, but the

couple simply didn't know how to close, or were afraid to hurt the other person's feelings or face their reaction. Some are afraid of the future, of being alone, and of having to deal with a deep sense of grief and loss. Many couples turn to a counselor or mediator at this point.

A good therapist should tell people who have reached this level the truth—that there's a good chance the relationship is over (at least for one of them)—but they rarely do. Keep in mind that a therapist is not paid to terminate a relationship. As long as the insurance provider pays, some therapists may continue "treating" the couple, even when the relationship is clearly terminal.

WHEN TO CALL IT QUITS

Are you currently in a dating relationship about which you have your doubts? How do you know when it's time to call it quits? First, you should consider whether the relationship is self-destructing internally or externally. Are the issues something you can control and work on, or are they not? While you may have used all the techniques taught in this book and made a sound pick, life has its curve balls and situations, and people can change. We hope that in unfortunate situations where calling it quits is the best solution, you'll follow our basic guidelines and end the relationship as quickly and painlessly as possible.

INTERNAL FACTORS THAT
SIGNAL QUITTING TIME

Internal factors are conditions that are present because you or your partner has changed or a significant life event has altered your relationship too much to put it back on track, despite outside support and internal efforts to change. There's so much hurt, anger, resentment, animosity, frustration, or control causing such a great degree of stress that the relationship is painful—**all the time.** Here's a breakdown of internal warning signs that indicate a strong need to close that relationship immediately and move on.

◇ **When the pain of staying in a relationship outweighs the pain of change, you'll change.** In a healthy relationship, the thought of losing your significant other is usually devastating. If losing your partner sounds like the better option, it probably is.

> 66 In a healthy relationship, the thought of losing your significant other is usually devastating. If losing your partner sounds like a great option, it probably is. 99

◇ **If you've separated two, three, or four times, received outside help both as a couple and as individuals, and find the relationship no better than it was before, it's time to leave.**

◇ **If there has been any physical, sexual, or psychological abuse without serious professional assistance and long-term follow-up.** It could be dangerous to your health. If another incident occurs, you should end the relationship immediately and again seek professional assistance.

◇ **When you're staying for the wrong reasons.** These may include a fear of being alone, fear that no one else will want you, worry over what others will think, fear of being unable to meet your financial obligations (financial hardship), custody visitation issues, religious convictions, or because you still think you can "change" your partner into the person you want or think he or she can be.

◇ **You have fallen completely out of love and your careers, lives, common interests, goals, ambitions, desires, and needs have moved to polar opposites.**

External Factors That Signal Quitting Time

External factors are conditions created outside of you and your control. Other people, events, and situations might create such intense pain and hardship that they are no longer tolerable. It can be a single traumatic event or a chronic situation, but is of a nature that's unacceptable or unresolvable. Here's a breakdown of external warning signs that indicate a strong need for seeking closure and moving on.

◇ **Baggage from "unfinished business" causes a major continuous disruption in your current relationship.** For example: a former partner stalks, harasses, intimidates, and/or destroys property. If your partner has failed to close this previous relationship properly by any means possible or bring the previous partner into acceptable behavior limits, it's time for you to move on.

◇ **Your partner had an intimate sexual encounter, relationship, or affair.** Once trust is gone, it's very difficult to recapture. It's like bathwater gone down the drain; even successfully plugging the tub won't bring it back. Chances are that you won't want it back once you determine it has gone bad.

◇ **A profound accident, illness, or external family pressure radically alters the relationship.** These conditions can create such intense hardship and change the relationship so drastically that any previous semblance of balance, happiness, or serenity you experienced has disappeared. Not everyone is cut out to be a saint, martyr, or personal savior, and none of us has a right to judge this very personal decision. This one is a judgment call. Each of us can only take so much.

◇ **An addiction remains unresolved or a relapse occurs.** The disease of addiction, regardless of what kind, can be threatening to lives, devastating to families, and damaging to children. The relationship is doomed if the addicted person refuses help to "consistently" recover.

◇ **Your children are suffering the consequences of your partner's unhealthy behavior.** We never have the right to make a child in our home suffer the consequences of unhealthy behavior at the hand of another adult, no matter how selfish or unselfish our motives for staying might be. We model our children's future. They deserve to be happy, healthy, and equally loved.

> **❝ Once trust is gone, it is very difficult to recapture. ❞**

 ## New Beginnings

So, you've escaped a bad relationship and are out on your own again. Now what?

It's time to re-program your concept of how successful connections are made and to lay the groundwork for the changes you need to enact to develop better picking skills. We have attempted to help you identify and resolve your core issues and conditions that may have kept you in and out of revolving-door relationships. From this point forward, we will offer new and insightful approaches to "picking" partners and developing healthy relationships, and will provide the tools you'll need to sustain a long-term productive partnership with the healthy man or woman you desire. This process begins in the next chapter.

Fifteen Minutes to Dating Smarter

Let's set the scene: It's 10:30 in the evening and you are heading out with several close single friends. It's been a long, tough week, and you've been solo and dateless for quite a while now. You've had a feeling lately that you're about to catch "The One." But to catch "The One," you must first meet "The One," and you sense that tonight might just be the night. How will you distinguish between the winners and losers or at least someone worth pursuing?

You may feel your dating skills getting sharper now that you're acquiring tools from this book. The prognosis is good for meeting someone who can be a healthy partner in a good relationship. How can you know whether someone is "The One" or just another unhealthy person in an attractive package? It's time to develop a good selection process. Below are tools you can use to weed out the losers so your next pick will be a winner.

In a nutshell, the **15-Minute Find** is a comprehensive interview technique that takes around 15 minutes and provides you with sufficient information to determine whether a person is worth pursuing or will probably be your next ex. As interviewer, you seek specific information from potential partners. Interviewees will have no idea they're being interviewed or that the information they're giving will help you determine how healthy a pick they are. You'll seek information in these five categories:

1. **Physical Chemistry**

2. **Communication Skills**

3. **Lifestyle and Interests**

4. **Parental-Educational-Geographic Influences**

5. **Relationship History and Closure History**

   The information you gather will quickly enable you to:

◇ Spot serious flaws, warning signs (Code Red Characteristics, or CRCs), and conditions in others that justify a quick escape.

◇ Differentiate a potential "friend" from a potential "mate." (A potential friend or a casual acquaintance will lack the qualities necessary for deep and lasting romance.)

◇ Identify enough positive characteristics to encourage your spending more time getting to know them in a dating situation so you can determine their potential for a successful long-term relationship.

※ THE S.T.A.R. OVERVIEW ※

The following represents the comprehensive model of the **15-Minute Find.** Each point of the star corresponds with one of the five

primary categories listed earlier. Within each category, we provide a breakdown to examine aspects of that area in greater detail. We explain why the category is important, list sample questions or strategies to elicit the responses you need, and show you how to analyze the answers and make a healthy decision. Once you learn how to use the information you'll gain, you'll be able to quickly ascertain whether someone you're considering dating has the qualities you seek.

Ideally, you'll want at least 70 percent (this figure is not set in stone!) of their responses to satisfy your minimum standards in choosing someone to date. Using this process determines whether they merit a *date*, not a marriage proposal. A safeguard in this process is noting the presence of "Red Flags." These may come in the form of multiple CRCs, unaddressed recovery issues, psychiatric conditions, recurring denial of repeated failure in relationships, nonacceptance of responsibility for previous failed relationships, inflexibility, close-mindedness, or poor communication skills. If major flaws exist, seriously consider skipping them as dating options, even if they scored more than 70 percent in all other areas or you're very attracted to them. An overriding flaw can be something that hooks your old issues, or a serious problem that can't be overcome. Beware!

The star operates in a clockwise manner, beginning with Physical Chemistry and Compatibility and ending with Relationship and Closure History. What you're ultimately searching for by using the 15-Minute Find is a **S.T.A.R.** (**S**omeone **T**rustworthy, **A**vailable, and **R**eal). No one point of the star can be excluded for the process to work properly.

The 15-Minute Find

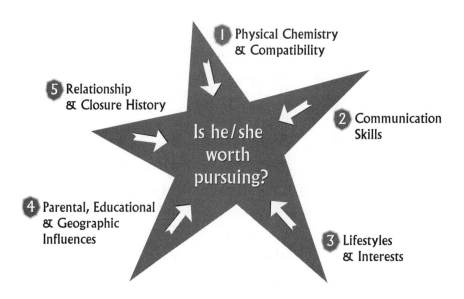

1. Physical Chemistry & Compatibility
2. Communication Skills
3. Lifestyles & Interests
4. Parental, Educational & Geographic Influences
5. Relationship & Closure History

Is he/she worth pursuing?

We break down each category into its subcomponents and provide specific information and examples (where appropriate) so you can easily understand how to use them to draw a comprehensive picture of a person you may date.

1 Physical Chemistry & Compatability

◇ **Physical attraction**

◇ **Sex appeal**

◇ **Mannerisms**

- ◇ **Dress**
- ◇ **Hygiene**
- ◇ **Déjà vu**

Initial
Contact

Physical Attraction

Do they catch your eye? Do you find yourself wanting a second, third, or fourth look? Do you have a nice little tickle in your stomach that's saying, "Wow!"? If "yes" answers are plentiful, physical chemistry is evident. Your hormones are kicking in ("Ooh, baby!"). Does your physical attraction checklist have several criteria that match? For example, you're attracted to blondes with a certain body-type, height, hairstyle, and flair. As you check your list, you're saying, "Yes, yes, no, yes, yes, yes." The "yes" responses, when compared to one "no," probably lead to an overall "yes." This process might be instantaneous or might take hours. Chances are if it takes hours to find attraction, you may be settling—or trying to convince yourself it exists.

If the person keeps looking back at you . . . and looking back at you, there's a good chance a connection is being made. Maintaining eye contact will increase the likelihood of contact. It also sends a clear signal that you're interested too. Before you ever approach a person, the probability is high that some physical attraction must be present to investigate further. In other words, whether you feel love at first sight or lust at first sight, it all begins with sex appeal. *Red Flag:* If the person is wearing a wedding ring, walking arm-in-arm with someone, or has a tan line circling their ring finger, chances are he or she is unavailable.

Sex Appeal

Ah, sex appeal. For you, Tommy Hilfiger, Donna Karan, or Polo might do it. Or maybe you favor cowboy boots, a leather mini-skirt, or a muscle shirt. You may love a layered look or a next-to-nothing one. With luck, they'll have what sexually appeals to you and vice versa. Some of you find a person dressed for success in a business suit appealing, while it could be a complete turnoff for others.

People's actions can also trigger an attraction or be sexy to you. They may be walking a dog, playing with a child, reading a book, participating in sports, attending a function, or spending quiet time alone with a musical instrument when you first notice them. Seeing that they share an interest of yours can be very seductive and alluring, especially if few others share that interest.

Mannerisms

How is their posture? Do they twirl their hair, bite their nails, or improperly control the volume of their voice? How tactful and engaging

are they in public? Which do you notice but find endearing? Are there any Red Flags (which would immediately send them down the express lane to "Gonersville")?

Dress

It's a black-tie affair with mostly single people. Your eyes are drawn to three standouts in the room. While most are dressed for success, you're trying to determine whether these nonconforming three are actually what they appear to be: a Klingon War Lord, Bozo the Clown, and a Marilyn Manson clone. You instantly eliminate them as possibilities based on the statements their appearance makes.

As you meet others, you may immediately notice a difference in lifestyle based solely on their attire. *Are they dressed appropriately for the situation or environment they're in? If not, is there a reason? Do they appear relaxed and comfortable or apprehensive as if putting on a facade? Does your style and taste mirror that of the person you're most attracted to or just the opposite?* Similar taste and style may equal similar interests, attitudes and comfort levels, but at times the reverse is true.

Hygiene

As you ride in a crowded elevator, you're immediately interested in an absolutely gorgeous guy or gal standing next to you. On your way to the 20th floor, you notice an odor that's stronger than fumes emanating from the back of a bus. On each passing floor, a few more fortunate people leave the elevator (escape!) and breathe a sigh of relief. Finally, you're alone with the object of your attraction, and realize that the aroma has also risen to the top. Despite the phenomenal looks, the gorgeous possibility plummets to the bottom of your interest list. You won't settle for romance that requires wearing a gas mask.

We all make strong and immediate judgments about people based on their hygiene and appearance, as do they about us. *Do they brush their teeth and groom themselves properly? Do they look as if they've slept or do dark circles under their eyes tell you they haven't? Are their clothes clean?* They might be able to get away with wearing the same undergarments two days in a row, but wearing the same outfit for days will be noticed.

Diet can have a great impact upon hygiene. People who overindulge in alcohol may smell like a brewery, however they try disguising it. Even those with the best hygiene might release a particular smell through their pores due to certain foods or spices they've eaten. And while a person may exude perfect hygiene in public, their home might smell like a litter box or look like an annex to the county dump.

Smells can leave lasting positive impressions as well. Have you ever spent intimate time with someone and smelled his or her heavenly scent on your clothes or towels for days afterward? This lasting good impression, called **Euphoric Recall,** is the combination of great chemistry and pleasant memory.

Déjà Vu

"Wow! You look, sound, and act exactly like my ex." There's a plus and minus side to déjà vu! The plus side is feeling an instant level of comfort and sense of familiarity with someone who reminds you of another person with whom you've previously felt a connection. You sense that you may have much in common, simply based on appearance, voice, style, and mannerisms. But you can't expect your new interest to be a carbon copy of the other person, or you'll set yourself up for failure. Trying to recapture old lost love through the similarities in a new one is apt to lead you to more disappointment.

The downside of déjà vu is that it might be connected to a less-than-positive memory. Be careful not to subconsciously transfer an old courtship attraction from a past lover to a new one. You may be living off the euphoria of courtship with the first. If that relationship had been successful and satisfying, you'd still be with the person.

Physical chemistry and compatibility require common sense, thought, and control of your emotions and hormones. While the initial contact sparks your interest (and it's imperative that chemistry is present), it's by no means the only quality you should rely on for assessing their potential as a partner. However, as the next four categories point out, your ability to maintain and enhance that chemistry is what will stand the test of time.

> 66 Trying to recapture old lost love through the similarities in a new one is apt to lead you to more disappointment. 99

2 Communication Skills

◇ **Eye contact**

◇ **Vocabulary**

◇ **Language skills:**
   Grammar
   Profanity
   Content

◇ **World aware**

◇ **Facial expression**

- ◇ **Continuous Confabulation**
- ◇ **Believability**

Eye Contact

You look up and your eyes accidentally meet his. Almost as a reflex you look away. Moments later, you glance back and it happens again. The third time you lock eyes and maintain eye contact for what feels like an eternity. Your heart is pounding. Finally, you tear yourself away, but not for long. You look again until he/she looks away. You've sent a clear signal that you're interested. It's time to initiate a connection or allow him to do so with you. This common scenario works the same in nearly every situation. Whether friends introduce the two of you or you make a connection at a business meeting, the first meaningful contact between two people is often through eye contact, and it can say a lot.

Some people, due to their nature, their job, or other circumstances, simply can't maintain eye contact when they're talking. Perhaps they simply lack the ability or the confidence to focus on you or it is not acceptable in their culture. However, an individual with darting, wandering, searching eyes probably is looking for someone else or is not satisfied with you.

Vocabulary

"Uh, um, you know, ah, know what I mean?" When a person is incapable of using or stringing together words over two syllables long, this can indicate a more serious problem. *Do they use appropriate words for appropriate situations? Do they answer open-ended questions that require more than a "yes" or "no" with just a few words? Does their vocabulary exceed yours—or does yours exceed theirs?* If you decide to date them, you'll communicate with them a great deal. Pay attention to the answers to these questions.

Language Skills: Grammar, Profanity, and Content

You can't say "ain't" because it ain't in the dictionary. *When you hear them speak, does their grammar reflect a higher or lower level of education than yours? Was their dinner last night an "eloquent affair" or "one heck of a spread with killer chow?" Do you feel as if you're listening to dialogue from an X-rated movie?* While some sporadic, tempered use of inappropriate language may be acceptable and understandable, their respect and sensitivity to your comfort level is most important. For example, "I feel like I'm paying a helluva lot of taxes" or "The President's speech was just a load of BS" might be acceptable expressions of their views, as they weren't intended to offend you. But this language is a part of their being. They express their passion for certain topics using certain words. Is their language acceptable to you?

Each person's tolerance level is a factor of his or her education and comfort level. Be aware that profanity in reference to someone's gender can be a warning sign that an underlying attitude or prejudice exists. "Why are all men jerks?" "She was such a bitch!" or "The bitch took everything I had." If they're willing to use such language in the initial stages of contact with you, imagine how their language will progress as your relationship does. People who gossip heavily or who readily judge others send a red flag that tells you to move on. If they gossip about others to you, they'll gossip about you to others—guaranteed.

The content of a conversation, above all else, will tell you about a person's character. If 90 percent of their conversations start with "I," they're discussing the person of utmost importance to them. But, if they consistently ask questions about you directed to you, they are attempting to get to know you, which is a very good sign. Conversations based solely around what *they* do, who *they* are, *their* career path, what *they* own, or on *their* likes and dislikes may indicate several things about them, such as:

◇ They're selfish and self-centered. ("I will only go to romantic movies. Action movies are always so contrived. I won't go see them.")

◇ They're probing to see if *you* can fit into *their* lifestyle. ("I play softball six nights a week. I really like having somebody come to watch me play.")

◇ They're trying too hard to impress. ("I plan to trade my Mustang in for a Jag.")

◇ They may lack the skills to effectively communicate on the opposite gender's level. ("I've never understood why women want us to talk about our feelings. What a bunch of crap.")

Ask yourself one final question: could they ever love another person as much as they seem to love themselves? An individual who focuses pri-

marily on you will in most cases have a healthy sense of who they are and well-developed communication skills. As they ask questions about you, they're most likely:

◇ Trying to get to know you more intimately.

◇ Searching for common interests, likes, dislikes, perceptions, and attitudes (or using the 15-minute Find on you!).

◇ Allowing you to talk about the topic you're most familiar with. (They know people feel better when they talk about themselves, and they want you to feel your best.)

World Aware

We're an information-hungry society that can't get enough from television, radio, newspapers, magazines, or the Internet. During a conversation you can quickly ascertain an individual's priorities and interests by the topics they initiate and discuss intelligently. A person's ability to absorb and grasp information is essential for them to understand and appreciate how it impacts their life and yours. While you may live far from Japan, its economy can have a direct impact on you. Failure to recognize current world issues can indicate blind ignorance or a lack of caring.

A lack of knowledge or an opinion of significant events such as the Columbine High School shooting, areas devastated by tornadoes or hurricanes, the Tiananmen Square tragedy, major wars, and so forth is evidence that a person has a closed mind, an uncaring attitude, or is intentionally isolated from society. While we can never know everything, some familiarity with local, regional, national, and world issues is important. Do you want to spend a great deal of time with a person who's locked in a vacuum without a clue?

Facial Expression

Is the person you're talking to suffering from a bad case of bitter beer face? Words can hide many feelings and emotions, but the face expresses many emotions: confusion, anger, confidence, happiness, depression, fear, hope, loneliness, infatuation, jealousy, boredom, anxiety, shyness, and shock. Do they smile, wink, grin, or blush at appropriate times? Can you see their face or is their make-up so thick you'd need to break through with a jackhammer to get a true glimpse? Does their face confirm, deny, or reciprocate your feelings? Their expressions are a dead giveaway of the true meaning behind their words.

Continuous Confabulation

Blah, Blah, Blah, Blah. . . . Chatty are they? Could they bore a monk? Are they going Mach 10 without a clue? ("Help, I am sitting in front of an idiot and can't get up!") Sense they aren't telling you the truth? Confabulation can mean either that they babble on pointlessly or are evading the truth with endless tongue-twisting that is at best difficult to follow or believe.

Believability

Combine all the data, observations, and content you've absorbed from a person, and you have your believability factor. Note any inconsistencies in their stories, the style and delivery of their message, or their sincerity. Above all, don't forget a sense of humor. The more you smile, the more they smile, and the better the chance you both have of "going the mile."

Now let's go beyond the initial contact and perception—and find out whether or not the person is a good candidate with whom to spend more time in the future.

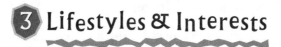

3 Lifestyles & Interests

◇ **Career History, Goals, and Income**

◇ **Work Schedule and Personal Time Management**

◇ **Hobbies and Interests**

◇ **Spiritual Beliefs**

◇ **Type of Friends and Time Spent with Them**

◇ **"Quirks"**

◇ **Taste and Style: Movies, Food, Music, Entertainment**

◇ **Habits: Good or Bad**

Interpersonal Compatibility

Career History, Goals, and Income

When a man and women meet for the first time, he'll tell her within 15 minutes what he does for a living, where he does it, and what he's good at. She'll tell him how she feels about that information, and about him, herself, or something else. Men, being task- and goal-oriented, view themselves by what they do. Women view themselves by their interactions with people—through emotional achievement, connection, expression or feelings. *Note:* Money matters! If your income is significantly greater or less than the income of the person in whom you're interested, it's essential that you discuss this topic within the first few dates. Money is among the top six causes of friction between couples (along with alcohol, sex, religion, children, and relatives), even those just starting out.

It's important to extract useful information as you need it. *Do your best to find out what kind of job they have, whether they enjoy it, and how long they've been there. If they have a history of changing jobs frequently, ask why. Do they tend to get fired? If so, why? Did they quit? Get promoted? Does their career require geographic mobility? Where do they want to end up? Do they have a career you can be supportive of and vice versa? Are you ready to date someone who's always on call? Are they ready to date you if you travel for a living?*

Work Schedule and Personal Time Management

Do they describe their 18-hour days as "the love of their life?" Do they have so much free time that he or she could become a pest? Will they have time for you? Do you work opposite shifts? Do they have children or parents who require special care or a great deal of their time? Will seeing each other once a month fulfill your concept of having a significant other? Does having them around seven days a week ("I'm all yours, all the time") make you want to enter a witness protection program?

You'd be surprised how many people pursue dates with someone whose schedule is difficult to work with. Had schedule difficulties been addressed in the beginning, they wouldn't have wasted time chasing work schedules only to discover their time incompatibility.

Hobbies and Interests

He plays golf; you love to cook. She plays tennis; you prefer to paint. She works on cars; you know they run on gas. He works out religiously; you like to shop until you drop. Ask plenty of questions about what they do to amuse themselves to learn whether their hobbies or interests are reasonably balanced with the expense and time it takes to pursue them. You need a clear picture of how serious they are about their pursuits to see whether your interests will balance with theirs.

Are you both interested in learning more about the other's hobbies and interests? (The key word here is *interested*, not obsessed!) Nine hours in front of the television, seven hours in front of a computer, or six hours a night playing video games doesn't leave time for healthy interaction with others. Five hours a night at the gym, six hours playing softball, or four hours volunteering at church provides them with interaction with others but little time to spend with you.

On the other hand, if they have few interests or hobbies (or maybe none at all), be careful. Either you'll become the primary focus of their attention (and will probably feel limited in pursuing your own interests), or you're on a fast train to Dullsville.

The values and beliefs reflected in their interests (or lack of interests) may mesh or conflict with yours. Only you can decide whether a relationship can work.

Spiritual Beliefs

Studies indicate that conflict over or compatibility with religious issues is the number one contributor to either the success or failure of a relationship. This is a sensitive subject to cover when you first meet someone. If you make even a casual mention of how you were raised, what religious values you practice, or what moral beliefs you hold, you can learn enough to know whether you are spiritually compatible.

Relationships with those who have views that are extremely different from yours will probably lead to unresolvable problems. Because religion and spirituality tend to be heartfelt and important core issues to share with your partner, this factor is significant. If a potential love interest doesn't share a belief that you hold dear, not only is having a complete relationship difficult, but the differing "visions" inevitably cause friction.

> 66 Studies indicate that conflict over or compatibility with religious issues is the number one contributor to either the success or failure in relationships. 99

We've noticed two things. One is that similar interests, ideals, and values regarding spiritual belief systems are essential to a successful relationship. The second is that failure to have a spiritual, religious, or belief system outside yourself is likely to yield what we refer to as **Self-Will Run Riot,** which is operating on your own will with no direction. Since people who lack active support systems aren't used to reaching out for help—whether therapeutic or spiritual—conditions often spiral out of control when a crisis does hit.

Type of Friends and Time Spent with Them

Once again, you can quickly find out whether a person has time and space in their life for you by exploring this area. *Do their friends have green, spiked hair or more piercings than a shish kebab? More ink on*

their bodies than we used in this book? (If that's your thing, too, no problem!) As they introduce you to their friends, you may see the disparity between your interest in football and theirs in splitting atoms. You might discover a huge difference between your lifestyle and that of their chosen friends. When you choose to blend two lives in a relationship, you get all that goes with each other's life, including long-term friendships, family, co-workers, and other people who are important to your partner—including that eccentric relative, messed-up ex, or demanding boss that everyone seems to have. The ability to be flexible, nonjudgmental, and accepting plays a large part in our ability to integrate ourselves into someone else's life.

Answering these questions will help you analyze potential partners' relationships. *What is their best friend like? Do they get along best with men or women? Have they had a lot of friends for a long time? What are their favorite activities with friends? If they've been "transplanted" to your area, are they making new friends? Is it an easy or arduous process for them? Where do they tend to meet new friends?* Whether they meet their friends at the gym, at work, or at the neighborhood bar can say much about their lifestyle. For example, a workout fanatic might be comfortable *only* in that situation.

Do plans involving you, whether tentative or confirmed, also include their friends? ("Sure, we'd love to meet you next Wednesday.") This can indicate that they're using friends as what we call an **Intimacy Defense Mechanism.** If they keep friends around at all times to avoid one-on-one contact with you, it may signal a lack of desire or confidence in their ability to interact with you on an intimate, one-on-one level. You may also be serving as a showpiece for them—they want you in their life for the sake of appearance, but not for intimacy.

Quirks

Is he 38 years old and still living with Mom? Does she have only one outfit or style of clothing? Has he developed his own personal, repetitive slang or language? ("Whatever!") Words or phrases unconsciously repeated over and over can drive you crazy.

Other habits may be important to them, but annoying to you: *She treats her shedding cat like a goddess and allows it to roam everywhere (even on the kitchen table!). He worships his stinky, stupid dog that chews up everything.* While some quirks are endearing, others aren't. Either kind may last a lifetime. Can you live with them for that long?

Taste and Style: Music, Food, Movies, Television, and Entertainment

She can't stand watching football, and you despise gardening and cooking shows. He likes Mexican; you prefer Chinese. She's a meat and potatos kind of gal; you're an organic vegetarian.

The key is discovery. Watch out! Any potential partner's tastes may be as varied as yours are. If you date, you'll spend a great deal of time doing various activities together. Are you both open-minded enough to test-drive each other's preferred ways of having fun? While Putt-Putt may be fun to you, their idea of a terrific activity may be going to a polo match. While you may not have previously enjoyed your love interest's favorite activities, you may find you enjoy them in his or her company. On the other hand, differences in activity preferences can cause dissension and leave you with a bad taste for sharing future activities.

During the courtship and infatuation stage, people tend *not* to voice their likes and dislikes for fear of scaring the other person off. They willingly trade sporadic unhappiness to feed the other's ego. Or they may let the other person's desirable qualities (looks, charm, money) cloud their judgment of the big picture. You may be willing to try an activity that

wouldn't normally interest you just to have a good-looking guy or gal on your arm.

With the 15-Minute Find, checking out this area is as simple as asking and sharing your likes and dislikes. Discussion up front will alleviate many potential problems down the road, especially when your date shows up with a parachute and you have an extreme fear of heights.

Habits: Good or Bad

You can smell your blind date, a chain smoker, eight feet away. Or, the aroma of alcohol streaming from the breath and emanating from the pores of this person nearly knocks you over. When you reluctantly oblige them with a good-night kiss, it's like running your mouth through a dirty ashtray. The date "stunk" from start to finish. Some people live with habits that others can't tolerate. Some people simply won't date those who smoke or drink; others date *only* those who are willing to indulge and "cut loose."

Of course, it's important to stay physically fit, but there's a fine line between taking fitness seriously and obsessing over it. Those who've gone to the fitness extreme frequently bring it into every aspect of their lives: diet, megavitamins, sleeping habits, perhaps even steroids. If you can "hang" with the heavyweights—good for you. But don't be surprised if your "buff beau or gorgeous gal" uses working out as an Intimacy Defense Mechanism. You may get close only if you're spotting for them during a workout.

Interpersonal Compatibility

What we've been discussing in this category is interpersonal compatibility. The investigation is aimed at comparing your interests to those of the person in whom you're interested. It's important that they meet your minimum standards for interpersonal compatibility before you accept a date or pursue several dates with the same person.

4 Parental, Educational & Geographic Influences (PEG)

◇ **Educational Background**

◇ **Parental Status**

◇ **Family of Origin Issues**

◇ **Divorce, Infidelity, and Recovery History**

◇ **Ethics, Values, Morals**

◇ **Cultural and Regional Factors**

Origin of
Influences
and Prior
Conditioning

Educational Background

Is it a neuro-cognitive brain dysfunction or brain damage? Acetylsalicylic acid or aspirin? Chateau Neuf du Pape or wine? Was she a Debutante Ball Queen the year you were King of the Pumpkin Festival? We all come from different worlds. The bottom line is how comfortable and accepting we are of the obvious differences.

Some think they can determine with whom they'll feel most comfortable by knowing their educational level ("degree of their degree"). This factor does have some merit. However, we know people with loads of letters following their names who have trouble holding a conversation. Others can't even correct the grammar in the Sunday comic section but have more people skills than the finest politician has. It's not impossible for two people with opposite backgrounds to find a common bond. However, level of education will to some degree dictate your interactions, style of living, income bracket, places you go, and the people you associate with.

People often want to date "up" in an effort to improve their stock in life. The key is not to focus too much on education, but to observe how people interact with others and carry themselves. A person without a college degree who dates a Ph.D. may not be able to discuss advanced astrophysics but may carry the flow of conversation in a social group. Another may be very well-read, yet quite content in their blue-collar career. *Intentionally* dating "down" can serve these not-so-healthy purposes:

> 66 The key is not to focus too much on education, but to observe how people interact with others and carry themselves. 99

◇ You're seeking an inferior, subservient partner who can be easily controlled.

◇ You're looking to satisfy wants or urges that are primarily physically or emotionally based.

◇ Your life is so complex, stressful, and taxed that you desire a less educated, less assertive person whom you feel will take little effort to maintain.

Ask simple questions. *Where did you go to school? Is the degree you have directly relevant to the job you have? How would you handle this situation? (Describe a hypothetical situation.)* Look for their level of common sense. Find out how much daily contact they have with people to get an idea of their people skills. Do they want to go back to school or did they do so? If they do, is it because they wish to learn and expand their abilities or because their job requires it? Listening to their vocabulary, content, comments on lifestyle, and what they've done provides much information on their education without deep probing.

Parental Status

Are your parents living or dead? To which parent are you emotionally closer? Where do your parents live? How often do you see them? What activities do you enjoy with them? How often do you talk with them? Do you have ex in-laws who are grandparents of your children? How often do you see them?

Questions such as these help you discover how connected potential partners are to their parents (whether living or dead), whether that connection is healthy, and what influences their parents had on them. Remember: You are how you were raised (see chapters 2 & 5).

Family of Origin Issues

Alcoholism, addiction, infidelity, depression, mental illness, abuse, neglect, obsessive-compulsive behaviors (relating to food, religion, or sex, for example), or any chronic, debilitating illness are touchier subjects that must be approached subtly rather than with straight-out questions such as these: *Is alcoholism present in your family? Was there ever a hostile divorce in your family?* To effectively broach these topics, here are several ways to allude to them. In a conversation, mention that you're going to visit someone close to you who has diabetes (or other chronic illness). They'll probably share similar experiences with you, after which you can ask whether there's a history in their family. "I'm celebrating my best friend's one-year anniversary of alcohol recovery with her." Again, you have created an in. You'll soon know if they have a similar experience to share. "I was thinking of volunteering at the hospital by taking people with depression and mental illness on outings. What do you think?" Once you've slipped mental illness into the conversation, follow up with questions that will elicit the information you need.

While knowing whether any of these issues are present is key, it's even more important to find out what they did or didn't do to resolve these family-of-origin issues. Presence of a serious issue doesn't immediately exclude them from being a pick, but it's critical that they've at least begun to address them. *Did they seek counseling? Have they been involved in a support or recovery program to address the effects on them? Are they still involved in recovery efforts? How long have they been dealing with these issues?* Failure to address, discuss, or admit to these issues, or denying their effects, is a clear warning sign. They'll bring their baggage and family issues directly to your doorstep if you let them. Walk away quickly!

Divorce, Infidelity, and Recovery Issues

We covered some of these issues above. This time, simply apply the guidelines we gave you earlier in the book on how to proceed with someone in recovery. If a person has less than five years of recovery for any issue addressed under Family of Origin, proceed with extreme caution. People are still prone to relapse, and primary issues are frequently far from resolved. Statistically, a person's odds for a permanent recovery get only slightly higher between one and five years; their chances dramatically improve after five years. Furthermore, our experience shows that recovering people rarely succeed in long-term relationships without at least a five-year consistent foundation.

How do you get information on divorce, infidelity, and recovery? Be as unassuming as possible, with a relaxed, even humorous, style. Show sincere interest in them. Deliver your questions matter-of-factly. They're much more likely to share sensitive information if they don't feel they're being interrogated. Reword our suggested questions into a style that works for you. You might ask, for example: *So, how did your last few relationships end? Why did you leave them? Why did they leave you? So, you've been divorced twice—tell me about your wives (or husbands). How did you meet them? Why didn't those marriages work out? Who called it quits?*

You may think these questions are too forward, but unless you're talking to a 45-year-old virgin, everyone has a history. Finding out how they've functioned with others gives you an idea what they'll do with you. If they mention ten affairs and five divorces—Danger, Will Robinson, Danger! Failure to ask these questions will result in a case of "We told you so!" As we said before, people are creatures of habit. If they don't address the unhealthy patterns by which they operated in previous relationships, they'll continue the same patterns with you.

Typically, both of you will have some divorce or difficult break-up experiences to share. You may express that your "stepparents were as wonderful to you as your real parents," which may encourage them to take the opposite stance about their stepparents. Or they may mention that their former in-laws see the grandchildren once a month, which tells you that they're no longer married but do have kids. A little common-sense sharing of experiences and hypothetical situations will get you a great deal of information without much difficulty.

Ethics, Values, and Morals

Because no other area can attract or repel you as quickly, it's important to learn a person's ethics, values, and morals right away. This represents the heart of their belief system and the principles by which they function. It's a deep reflection of their character, the passion behind their beliefs, the motor behind their motives. If you're a devout Democrat and meet a radical Republican, will your views on an issue such as abortion be diametrically opposed? How do you feel about that possibility? Although you need not have the same value system, the more you have in common, the more likely your relationship will stand the test of time.

Ethics refer to people drawing appropriate lines, staying within them, and performing to acceptable standards. They're rules we follow to respect another person's boundaries and decisions we make that reflect our character.

Ethics are actions we attempt to practice in our daily lives, such as respect and honesty that are based upon our morals and our view of right and wrong. Morals are the strongly held beliefs, feelings, judgments, and boundaries that guide our thoughts and behavior. Examples of morals are, "I believe in telling the truth." "My relationship with God comes first." Examples of ethics are actions such as telling the truth even

> ❝ Morals are the strongly held beliefs, feelings, judgments, and boundaries that guide our thoughts and behavior. ❞

if it will be painful, returning a lost wallet to its owner, or practicing your faith by serving others.

Values are simply what you prioritize as important to you within your ethics and morals. Money may be at the bottom of your list while taking in strays and being kind to animals might be near the top. The more detailed your discussion of important values, the greater your sense and identification of what their values are in relation to yours. If you say what's important to you and they are not similarly enthusiastic, this is a sign that you lack common ground. Common ground creates mutual enthusiasm.

Cultural and Regional Factors

Texas chili and oysters on the half shell are not exactly common ground. The rodeo is a long way from Broadway. Is your ideal evening taking in the symphony while theirs involves front-row tickets at a rock concert? Our ideas of fun, fantasy, and flavor vary as do our backgrounds. Were you raised where seasons change, while they've never seen snow? Regional differences can be an exciting discovery or a troublesome obstacle.

Extremely different values can significantly affect how easily two people find middle ground. A big-city girl may expect a relationship to progress at a much different pace than a southern, country gentleman might expect. Living with someone from the West Coast might be completely unacceptable to a person from the Bible Belt. No matter how open-minded we might be, we must still consider a person's background and our ability to merge our lifestyles.

5 Relationship & Closure History

◇ **Marital Status**

◇ **Detailed Chronological Closure History and Types of Previous Picks**

◇ **Longevity of Relationships and Status with Former Partners**

◇ **Time Since Last Relationship**

◇ **Causes and Conditions of Relationship Failure**

◇ **Sexual Preference and History**

Long-Term Relationship Capability

Marital Status

You might ask: *What an unusual tan line you have on your left ring finger. That gold band wouldn't stand for anything important, would it?* Or you might hear: *My marriage license is only good in the state in which I live; I don't recognize reciprocity. I am getting a divorce. I'm leaving her/him soon.* A legitimately available single (currently unmarried/uncommitted/completely divorced) person is what you should be looking for. If people are hesitant to give you their phone number or e-mail address, or tell you in what part of town they live or where they work, they're either hiding a significant other or aren't convinced they should divulge this information to you so quickly. If they're still hesitant three months later, it's more likely they have a significant other. Simply ask the question, "Are you single?" When in doubt, refer to *How to Spot a Liar* in chapter 3 for all the information you should need. If necessary, it's relatively simple and inexpensive to have someone's background checked.

Detailed Chronological Closure History and Types of Previous Picks

In the course of conversation, a great question to ask is: *What kinds of people have you dated in the past?* Then follow up with questions designed to elicit more detail: *Were they older or younger than you? How did you meet them? Did you have a lot in common with the people you dated or did you tend to find your opposite?*

From the picks they've described, can you tell whether their Picker is broken? Sure you can! You can tell when someone is controlling. If a person continually says that they chose people who controlled them, they have a Broken Picker we call The Girdle (see chapter 2). If they indicate that everyone they dated was seriously wounded, damaged, or needy, they have a Broken Picker we refer to as M.A.S.H. In other words, if you are healthier than their picking pattern indicates, they

won't be interested in you for long—and you won't want them either. (Give them a copy of this book to read and tell them to call you in six months—after they've seen a therapist.)

Termination Techniques

Probably the most important question in this category is: *How did your previous relationships end?* You want to discover how they break up in a relationship, what their closure modus operandi is. Do they handle it in a forthright manner or rely on a less-than-honorable method of closure? The following are some more common tactics people use to end a relationship.

⬦ **The Fade Away:** This person allows a relationship to disintegrate by avoiding you and thus avoiding the conflict.

⬦ **The Executioner:** You're history—right now—and you're told why. You've been declared "guilty" and have no chance to defend yourself. They refuse contact, refuse discussion, and carry out your sentence immediately. *(Would the next victim please report to the chopping block?)*

⬦ **The Western Union:** You get a letter, e-mail, or note telling you that absence didn't make the heart grow fonder. You were out of sight, then out of mind, and have been replaced by a new find.

⬦ **The Shattered Glass:** The relationship is smashed when one party "accidentally" gets caught with his or her "pants down." You unexpectedly catch them engaging in intimate interaction with someone at a restaurant or event, in the bedroom, or in some unexpected place.

⬦ **The Gravedigger:** These people invite you to your own relationship funeral, at which they recall all your flaws and shortcomings as well as details of how you ruined their life. They bury you under an avalanche of blame and guilt.

- ◇ **The Freezer:** What was once warm and caring is now cold and callous. Conversations become shorter and shorter, physical contact non-existent, and their calendar suddenly fills with a spot for everyone but you.

- ◇ **Pavlov's Dog:** The relationship is over, but the sex lingers. There's no heart, no emotion—but mutual physical satisfaction persists at the coldest level.

- ◇ **Military Max:** You're involved in a "kill or be killed" war. Unique weapons such as anger, hostility, revenge, gossip, threats, and intimidation aren't camouflaged at all. The result is massive casualties to all involved—the two warring parties and their friends, family, children.

- ◇ **The Saboteur:** These people terminate by doing things they know you won't tolerate. Setting up the relationship for failure may take time, but they'll always succeed in passing the responsibility for ending the relationship to their partner.

- ◇ **Out of Gas:** The relationship started out like a ride in a Ferrari—a lean, mean passion machine. You wound up on a bicycle built for two, both pedaling in the same direction for a brief ride to friendship. When the passion was gone, somebody said, "So long!"

- ◇ **Oil and Water:** A relationship where the couple should have remained "friends only" but forcibly crossed the line to passion/love, will terminate badly! Whereas great lovers may turn out to be great friends, not all great friends were meant to be great lovers!

- ◇ **The Revolving Door:** "We're done." "No, were not." "This time it's for real." "For sure it will be next time." "This time I'm serious" (or was it last time?) Their ex pops up more than a jack-in-the-box. They are in and out of a past relationship so many times that you need a calculator to keep score.

- ◇ **Rescue 911:** They wouldn't stop calling, writing, stalking, abusing, or harassing you, so you called upon a greater authority, the legal system, to terminate the relationship for you.

◇ **Mutual Resolution:** Things didn't work out and you mutually discuss open, honest, tactful, and amenable way to call it quits.

Try getting more than just the history of their previous relationships. How were they closed? Finding out how the one prior to their meeting you ended might tell you just one closure tactic they used based on the type of pick they made. Delving deeper will show you whether or not they have a pattern when it comes to relationship closure tactics.

Longevity in Relationships and Status with Former Partners

Determine how long their average relationship lasted, what influence relationships had on them, and how close they are to previous partners. *Are you still friends with your ex? Do you have children? How often do you see your former wife/husband, boyfriend/girlfriend? How long were you dating/married?* Do your best to determine whether their relationships typically lasted less than a month, three to six months, or a longer. Are they a miler or a quarter horse?

We must pay attention when someone has a pattern of short- or long-term relationships. When their consistent history has been in and out of short romances, you know one of two things.

1 They have a very Broken Picker and have to bail fast.

2 They have flaws that drive their picks away.

Ending of long-term relationships might be explained in one of three ways:

1 They might have issues with co-dependency, relationship addiction, or victim issues. They perhaps pick poorly but stay too long because they're unhealthy, which compounds damage to themselves.

2 They may stay in a "desert" situation for the wrong reasons.

3 They had a long-term investment in a relationship that went bad due to the other person. They got out in a reasonable time or tried to resolve the problems without success. These people may be new to the dating scene because of being involved for so long. These types might be healthier than the average person—just victims of poor circumstances.

Find out their status with former partners. *Do they have reasonable, acceptable, and legitimate boundaries?* You can't be expected to quit your job just because you work with someone you dated a few years back. Being friends is okay; being overly friendly is not. When children are involved, it's best that a relationship focuses on your common interest—your children. The children can then observe a relationship that models a friendship with shared responsibilities and concerns. Watch for signs of a hostile ex who might eventually intimidate, threaten, or bring in the legal system should *you* eventually break up with him or her.

Time Since Last Relationship

This category is short and sweet. *Are they playing leapfrog by jumping from person to person to person, or have they gone into hiding since closing their last relationship? Are they currently dating more than one person? If they came out of a long-term relationship, how long has it been since they dated someone else? Have they had sufficient healing time?* This often depends on whether or not they were the "breaker" (initiated the breakup) or the "breakee" (got dumped). Breakers know that the end is near so they have opportunity to prepare themselves and even to initiate a relationship with someone else. Thus, they often need less time to heal. Breakees might need more time to heal because they had little to no warning that termination was imminent thus are frequently devastated. They feel profoundly rejected as the breaker basically stated that they are undesirable and no longer welcome in their life, perhaps without even giving a reason.

Causes and Conditions of Relationship Failure

If explanations regarding why and how they closed their previous relationships don't ring true to you, or if they always point a finger at someone else, rationalize everything, and take no responsibility, consider whether they're waving a red flag that foreshadows what you can expect in a relationships with them. By now you should be able to spot such warning signs as they surface.

Sexual Preference and History

You're a girl. He's a boy. Make sure he likes girls. If not, he's your competition, not your next date. The reverse to this scenario is also true. If you prefer heterosexual (rather than homosexual, bisexual, or other), it's a good idea to make sure someone you regard as a potential partner does too. You can save a lot of embarrassment as well as avoid wasted time chasing a lost cause or serious project.

> 66 Sex shouldn't be the focal point of your 15-Minute Find investigation. 99

By now you've asked many questions about their dating history and should be able to surmise how sexually active they've been without asking directly. If they've talked about not having a date for quite awhile, they've either gone without sex or don't consider a one-night stand a date. If they're jumping from date to date, sex is either *not* an issue or the *only* issue, or they could be Gunslingers putting notches on their belt.

Sex shouldn't be the focal point of your **15-Minute Find** investigation. However, responsible investigation would include issues such as their opinion on STDs, birth control, and their opinion on safe sex protection. More on this in chapter 7.

✳ EXPECTATIONS AND TIMETABLE FOR USING THE 15-MINUTE FIND ✳

We know it took you longer than 15 minutes to read the 15-Minute Find but we expect that you'll use only what applies to your particular situation. Our main purpose was to offer you a choice of tools for making smarter dating decisions.

You might be asking yourself, "Is this too much to go through to sift out the losers from the winners?" No. The first time you use the 15-Minute Find, it will probably take longer and may feel like an overwhelming task. But the more you practice, the better you will get at executing the process. Use friends, family, and colleagues as guinea pigs. Not only will you have fun practicing and improving your 15-Minute Find technique, but you'll get to know those on whom you practice better and possibly will improve the quality of those relationships. Should they know they're being "used" for practice? Absolutely not. It wouldn't be the same if they knew. You're simply trying to make a successful, healthy connection with another person.

7

Make Them Want You

Bubba's Daily Planner

Lisa's Daily Planner

It's 7:15 P.M. on Friday night, at 204 Clueless Court. Bubba has a 7:30 P.M. date with Lisa, who lives 11 minutes away. In his mind, 4 minutes is plenty of time to fix up what's already impressive—Bubba. He stands in front of his mirror wearing the same underwear he's worn for the past three days. But because tonight is special (he might just get lucky!), inside out they go. Next, he reaches into the pile on the floor for the pair of jeans that appears to be the cleanest. His shirt is relatively clean, despite the wrinkles. Even though he took a shower, there was no time to shave ("Heck, it's only two days' growth!"). He heads out the door, ready to impress his future ex. As he arrives at Lisa's place, he's suddenly inspired by her neighbor's rose bushes. As he whips out his pocketknife and cuts a half-dozen red ones, he thinks: "I'll really impress her now!"

On the same day at 605 Looker Avenue, Lisa is pumped. After meeting Bubba at work, she immediately thought, "This could be the one." He was looking so good and passed the 15-Minute Find at their initial meeting. On the way home from work, she picked up her dry cleaning, had her hair and nails done, and purchased some accessories to go with her new outfit. When she arrived home at 4:30 P.M., she only has three hours to go before her date. She's since changed clothes 27 times before deciding on an outfit (she's still not sure it's perfect). Lisa has a bad case of mirroritis, which mainly affects women. She simply can't pass a mirror without seeing something she has to change. No matter how good she looks (she never thinks she looks as good as she does), she worries that she won't look just right. That's why Bubba has been waiting outside for 20 minutes!

When that front door opens, will Lisa and Bubba get what they're expecting? Let's examine each scenario in terms of what each person is trying to achieve and what the outcome is likely to be.

⊗ IS WHAT YOU SEE WHAT YOU GET? NOT ALWAYS! ⊗

Bubba has delusions of grandeur. While he knows how to operate and dress for success at work (where he met Lisa), his social life can definitely use refining. He's a nice guy with a great personality and wonderful intentions but is rough around the romantic edges.

Lisa, on the other hand, knows how to prepare but goes overboard. She aspires to be stunning and perfect. Her high expectations are out of

proportion to the reality of the situation. In fact, she went to such in-credible measures to be the object of her date's desire that she failed to be herself—the relaxed, lovely, and easygoing woman to whom Bubba was attracted in the first place. Her inquisitive, light-hearted questions (some of which came from the *15-Minute Find*) attracted him. Bubba felt she had a genuine interest in "him," and was never aware of being interviewed for tonight's date.

When the front door opened, both were shocked by what they saw. Because there was no discussion about where they were going and what they would do, Bubba had prepared for a date with the person he met at work, while Lisa prepared for a date with the man she longs for. An ounce of proper preparation could have prevented this pound of disap-pointment and embarrassment. While the basic components for a good connection between Lisa and Bubba still exist, they need to spend more time together so they can become better acquainted and get on the same wavelength. But, if they don't make it past this first date, that won't happen.

ROMANCE ETIQUETTE

You might be wondering why the 15-Minute Find didn't seem to work. Picking a good date is not enough; the trick is to have the date it-self go well. Bubba and Lisa failed to follow up their picks with proper preparation and sufficient Romance Etiquette in mind.

Here we offer some Romance Etiquette guidelines that should get you and your next healthy pick off to a flying start. Heeding these point-ers will give you the greatest opportunity for success by helping you im-press your next date rather than regress into your old ways.

Put Yourself in Tip-Top Dating Shape

◇ **Watch less television.** The relationship you fantasize won't become reality until you stop watching television romances and start working on your own. Addressing the causes and conditions of your previous failures will hopefully prevent you from failing again. What you've read so far and learned from the exercises in this book should already make you more attractive to healthy people.

◇ **Stay current.** Be able to carry on an articulate conversation, no matter what the topic. While expertise on every topic would be a turnoff, the more intelligent your dialogue, the more interesting you'll appear.

◇ **Keep fit.** You're composed of a body, mind, and spirit that are more attractive when you're mentally, physically, and spiritually healthy. You are what you eat and what you "digest" in other ways.

◇ **Be honest and sincere.** Games and barriers waste time. Healthy relationships simply won't develop out of a false presentation. No matter how hard you pretend to be someone else, you'll eventually return to who you really are, leaving the person you're with questioning whether you're person A or person B. Let your expectations and goals for the relationship be known.

◇ **Actively listen.** Really hear what others say and specifically react to what you've heard. Avoid preparing your response as the other person speaks. As the old saying goes: "We have two ears and only one mouth so that we can listen twice as much as we speak." We respond best to those who listen to us as though we're the most important person in the room at that moment.

◇ **Think and anticipate but don't assume.** Carefully plan what, when, and how your date should go and then let each other know. This can be done by both individuals as a team or by alternating romantic responsibilities. Consider what it might cost and who is covering the expense. Have several options in mind so you can choose what interests both of you. At the same time, be open to new experiences and dare to be different. A brief discussion will prevent your showing up for a picnic wearing a suit. The more questions you ask, the less you'll have to rely on assumptions.

◇ **Confirm your date.** You may have met briefly, quickly exchanged phone numbers or e-mail addresses, and decided to go out. It's important to confirm that you're still interested in going out and are looking forward to the time you'll spend together. Your date will be impressed that you took time to be considerate, and will appreciate knowing that you were thinking about him or her. How far in advance should this contact be made? It depends on how much time falls between the day you met and your first date. The less time between the two, the quicker you should call someone after meeting them. If a date is weeks away, calling a week or so before is appropriate and appreciated.

> 66 The beginning phase of dating someone new is a process of discovery, not finality. 99

◇ **Have reasonable expectations, and be tactful.** Expect to have a good time on your date, but don't have unrealistic expectations about the person or the outcome of the date. The beginning phase of dating someone new is a process of discovery, not finality. Everyone can have a bad day or be nervous early in a relationship. Extend the same consideration to others that you'd like them to give you. Create some mystery by evading the infamous first kiss (gasp!) or other physical intimacy on the first date. While you're treating them with respect and keeping the pace comfortable, you're also placing a question in their mind about whether or not you find them attractive. A little sexual frustration, tension, and mystery can be very enticing.

◇ **Follow up your date.** Whether you had the date of a lifetime or a date that seemed to last a lifetime, make closure. If it went well, closure may mean scheduling another date. If it was a catastrophe, closure means a tactful and gracious "good-bye."

◇ **Obey the speed limit.** When meeting people who are close to your date (family, friends, colleagues, or employers), be friendly yet respect their boundaries. Be gracious, have a sense of humor, keep conversations light and brief, and express an interest in who they are and what their relationship to your date is, especially if you're meeting a parent or employer. Avoid talking about the pace or direction of your relationship (your date may have a different perception!).

◇ **Don't delay communication.** Don't hesitate or be afraid to ask someone out. Every day you fail to approach a person to whom you're attracted is a day he or she might meet someone else and never get to know you. If you used the 15-Minute Find, communication went well, and you landed a phone number or e-mail address, use it! The person is probably interested in you, too. In the early process of dating, problems should be brought up immediately. Be tactful. Don't worry about damaging a relationship early by telling the truth. If you fail to address a crucial issue, you're delaying the inevitable. The more honest and upfront you are, the smoother things will go in the long haul. But again, be tactful.

BE "THE TOAST" RATHER THAN BECOME "TOAST"

Here we offer some tips on how you can make a lasting first impression.

1. **Toast:** To celebrate in honor of a person. To applaud extraordinary spirit or achievement or be held in high esteem.

2. **TOAST (Typically Offensive and Stupid Terminators):** A self-destructive act by which you burn your chance for relationship success. These often happen early in the dating process and are easily avoidable.

People often make stupid, thoughtless, and fatal mistakes early in the dating process that can unnecessarily end a relationship before it even gets started. You may be aware of TOASTs and know that you use them, or you may not realize it at all. Make a conscious effort to recognize, avoid, and correct these behaviors.

Here are ten TOAST examples to avoid if you want to survive the "cut."

1 **Don't let your smell beat you to your date.** Bathe! We mean with soap and water, preferably on the same day as the date. Deodorant was a fine invention—use it! Take it easy on cologne and perfume. If your breath can peel paint, may we suggest a toothbrush—with toothpaste?

2 **Two is company. Three's a crowd.** Group hug? Not today! If they wanted to date your friends, roommate, or co-workers, they'd have gotten their phone numbers, too. They want to go out with (and get to know) *you* so don't make it a party. With one-on-one, the focus is on each other. You're an adult so it's not necessary to bring a chaperone. If safety is a concern, however, meet in a public place like a restaurant or mall. Let a friend know where you're going, with whom, and when you expect to be home.

3 **Choose a dating activity that will allow you to have the best time together.** Three hours in a darkened theater without talking is not a good way to get to know someone. Taking your date, who is a vegetarian, to a steakhouse won't impress him any more than if you starve him. Taking your date to a double-header baseball game when it's 95 degrees with 90 percent humidity won't thrill her as much as the fantastic water park across the street.

4 **Be on time.** Being late says, "I'm not that interested in impressing you." Need we say any more? Canceling a date at the last minute, short of having a really, really good reason, is unacceptable. It's like ordering your favorite meal at a restaurant only to be told that the particular item is not available. Your expectations were heightened, then crushed. Pay attention. Chronic cancellations could account for your single status. Those in a profession that requires them to be "on call" should make sure their date fully understands their working situation and the limitations it places on them.

> 66 People like to talk about themselves because they think they know the subject well. 99

5 **If you use too much "I" and "Me," you'll never get to say "We."** If you dominate a conversation with the word "I," the relationship will surely die. People want to learn indirectly how wonderful you are, not hear it directly from you. Being a legend in your own mind will bore your date and prove you wrong. If you constantly talk about yourself, you'll learn nothing about your date. On the other hand, people like to talk about themselves because they think they know the subject well. Give them a chance to talk!

6 **Don't oversell.** While people love hearing how wonderful they are, a constant barrage of compliments can make them uneasy. If you constantly praise a date in an effort to "close the deal," he or she won't perceive you as real. Your credibility will be questioned, as they won't be able to differentiate between a true compliment and a butter-up line. Most people realize that being "perfect" is a state of mind, not a state of being.

7 Better to remain silent and be thought a fool than to speak and remove all doubt. Okay, the conversation has stopped and silence has crept in for what feels like an eternity. The discomfort is unbearable so you end it by saying, "Um . . . Duh . . . Er . . . Boy, you've got a hot sister." "In your picture, it looked like you had more hair." "You should try this teeth-whitener I use. What a difference it would make."

So how does your foot taste? Saying something incredibly dumb to end long, awkward periods of uncomfortable silence will make you wish that the silence was never broken. Think before putting your mouth in motion.

8 Call your date by the correct name. Bill is not spelled M-i-k-e. Janet is not spelled K-a-r-l-a. Calling your date by the wrong name will make them question their fate. They'll wonder: Are you indeed over your ex? Is this simply a rebound romance for you? Are you seeing someone else as well? Calling your date by the wrong name could leave you with a cold fish—even though you ordered a hot, juicy steak.

9 Intense PDA (Public Displays of Affection) is far from okay. You're hanging on to them like a leech on a carcass. You're trying to do a tonsillectomy without using your hands, when a peck on the cheek is more appropriate. You went out with a person but ended up with a blind octopus that handled your body like an encyclopedia written in Braille. An hour into your date, did you wish you were wearing a garlic-laced necklace or cross as your Dracu-date seemed to devour you for his evening meal? While passions may be running high for both of you, others have to endure your PDA. Show some class.

10 **The showdown doesn't have to mean show time.** The date has gone well. Pressure is on for a fantastic finale. Flow with it rather than freak out. People seldom remember who broke the ice; they're just happy to be standing in a puddle. Let your first kiss be as easy and comfortable as the process that led to it. Don't make it a huge production or run away in fear (see "Bad Kissers" at the end of this chapter).

In Through the Out Door

You've used the 15-Minute Find and found someone worth pursuing. He (She) is delicious to perfection—gorgeous, handsome, smart, humorous, and sensual. It's date two (or three or . . .) and you're having a ball. You've been out several times and feel comfortable springing something fun on your newly found interest. You're sitting casually in your living room and would like to probe a bit deeper without coming on too strong. You'd like to read between their lines. We have the perfect exercise for you to use. It can be done either openly or not. For a change, it's much easier and even more fun to do with their knowledge.

This exercise is modeled after the Johari Window, which was first introduced by Joseph Luft in his 1969 book entitled *Of Human Interaction* (Palo Alto, CA: National Press). The four panes of the Johari Window represent the conscious, subconscious, secret, and blind (all parts of the personality) for the purpose of looking at a person's personality tendencies and characteristics. More than anything else, it's fun and accurate more often than not.

If you're ready, get paper and a pen. Follow the instructions without hesitation or analysis. There are no wrong answers. It's important that you write down the *first* thought that enters your mind, as this will be

WAYS MEN CAN IMPRESS WOMEN

◇ **Practice appropriate chivalrous behavior.** Be a gentleman (gentle + man) and take care of her needs without prompting. Open doors, offer your coat when she's cold, etc.

◇ **Be strong, yet not abrasive.** Women don't react well to a spineless jellyfish that won't stand up for himself, but be careful not to cross the fine line between confidence and cockiness.

◇ **Express and ask about feelings.** A woman appreciates a man who is willing to talk about his feelings and is sincerely interested in hers.

◇ **If you're consuming alcohol, keep it social and minimal.** If you have to be "fortified" with alcohol to be with her, she'll sense you can't relate to her sober.

◇ **Exhibit confidence, not jealousy.** The reality that she'll stay in contact with friends and acquaintances she had before she met you shouldn't threaten you.

◇ **Be accountable for your words and actions.** Be a man of your word and let your actions show your intentions and character.

◇ **Realize that relationships can't be bought.** Keep things simple. While it's nice to be spoiled, little things are often much more appreciated and sincere. Buy her a card, not a car.

◇ **Treat her with the same courtesy, respect, and enthusiasm in front of your friends, family, and colleagues as you do in private.** Consistency counts. If she's your "girlfriend" in private, she should be your "girlfriend" in public, not just your "friend."

WAYS WOMEN CAN IMPRESS MEN

◇ **Avoid facades.** Don't hide behind makeup, clothing, and accessories. Men want to recognize the woman they met today when they meet via serendipity next week. Men respond well to a woman with class and respect her to the degree that she respects herself.

◇ **Strike a balance between independence and reliance.** Men want to know that they're needed, but aren't looking for glue-woman. Attract him with some elusiveness and he'll want what he thinks he can't have.

◇ **Don't overanalyze him or situations.** Often a man's simple answer is exactly what he means and should be taken at face value. Don't read between the lines.

◇ **Make a quick, firm decision.** Men are task- and goal-oriented, therefore a clear decision leads in a definite direction.

◇ **Don't ask loaded questions.** A "loaded" question asks for the answer you want, rather than for an honest answer. Examples are: "Do I look fat in this outfit?" "Do you think she's prettier than me?" Whatever answer you get can be manipulated, distorted, and held against them for the next millennium.

◇ **Allow him to treat you like a lady.** Give him parameters and indicate when you appreciate his efforts or when he's gone too far. (It worked for Pavlov's dogs, didn't it?)

◇ **Be on time.** If you make him wait, he'll think he's not important or that you don't value promptness. He got there on time to impress you. Let him.

◇ **Be comfortable with his friends without going too far.** Men appreciate women who get along well with their friends. They'll draw the line, however, if they perceive that you're flirting or cheating.

◇ **Periodically initiate physical intimacy.** Whether it's a hug, kiss, holding hands, or more, it makes a man feel desirable, special, appreciated, and wanted.

◇ **Tell it like it is from the start.** Clearly express your expectations regarding the pacing of the relationship and physical intimacy. From a man's perspective, knowledge beats trial and error every time.

your truest and most accurate answer. Number your paper one through four and place three bullets (or dots) under each number, as shown below. Each answer requires one word only so you don't need a lot of space. (We assume you'll take the exercise before giving it to anyone else so you'll know how it works and what your own answers are.) We'll lead you through the exercise so you'll be able to do the same for others.

QUESTION NUMBER ONE: YOUR FAVORITE ANIMAL

Instructions: Write down your favorite animal. If you don't have one, choose a type of animal (living, stuffed, animated, etc.) for which you have a fondness. List the three *personality* characteristics that best describe your favorite animal next to the dots beneath it. For example, if you chose a dog, rather than writing that it has fur, a tail, and a cold wet nose (which we already know), write one-word descriptions that best exemplify that animal's personality (see the example below).

1. Dog

◇ Loyal

◇ Powerful

◇ Loving

QUESTION NUMBER TWO: YOUR FAVORITE COLOR

Instructions: Write down your favorite color, even if it's a shade of a more primary one. Imagine yourself sitting in a room for a few minutes, surrounded by your favorite color. The walls, ceiling, floor, and furniture—everything is that color. List three single words that best describe

how being surrounded by your favorite color makes you feel (see the example below).

2. Blue

◇ Happy

◇ Warm

◇ Secure

QUESTION NUMBER THREE: YOUR FAVORITE BODY OF WATER

Instructions: Write down your favorite body of water. It could be any body of water, such as an ocean, lake, river, moat, lagoon, waterfall, pond, pool, hot tub, bath tub, sink, toilet, puddle, eyedropper—whatever floats your boat (pun intended!). List three one-word characteristics of your favorite body of water that aren't already known. Don't say, for example, that the ocean is blue, cold, and wet.

3. Waterfall

◇ Intense

◇ Refreshing

◇ Continuous

QUESTION NUMBER FOUR: YOUR MOST BEAUTIFUL SCENE

Instructions: Imagine yourself in a room with huge window but no door. As you look out that window you see the most beautiful scene, person, or event you could ever imagine. It could be anything—a sunrise, sunset, mountain, waterfall—and as elaborate as you want. As you

look out that window—*poof, it's gone!* You'll never see it again and will never leave the room. List three single words that best describe how you feel about the loss of that scene (if you view it as a loss at all).

4. A Hawaiian Sunset

◇ Frightened

◇ Angry

◇ Depressed

Because it is possible (though rare) that you did not see it as a loss, here's a second example:

4. A Hawaiian Sunset

◇ Thankful

◇ Serene

◇ Spiritual

It's fine if some of your answers corresponded to or were similar to ours, or were repeated to some degree from one section to another.

ANALYZING YOUR ANSWERS TO "IN THROUGH THE OUT DOOR"

Let's review what your answers mean.

Question Number One: Your Favorite Animal

Your favorite animal represents *how you think other people see you.* To prove our point and show you how others may be perceiving you, think about the number of times you've seen someone playing with their pet and thought to yourself, "That guy looks exactly like his dog" or

"That woman resembles her cat." People frequently choose their pets based on an image they want to project to others. For example, you see a man in his twenties walking down the street with a spike-collared Doberman pinscher named "Killer" at his side. What image is he trying to project? Is your first perception that he is an aggressive, dominant, powerful, aloof, commanding, independent, tough-guy, bad-boy? Across the street a young woman about the same age walks by with a cock-a-poo she calls Precious Princess Penelope. What image does she project? Energetic, feminine, playful, prissy, loyal, cute, loving, friendly?

While these perceptions aren't 100 percent accurate, we've found more often than not that they're very close. Projection error can, however, occur. You may incorrectly attribute characteristics to a person based on previous experiences. Prior imprinting may bias your perceptions. The Doberman owner could be a gentle, caring, passive individual who simply likes the breed, while the cock-a-poo owner could be popping anti-depressants and anti-psychotic tranquilizers to keep from having another meltdown.

Question Number Two: Your Favorite Color

Your favorite color represents *how you see yourself.* This can be a simple reflection of a person's self-esteem. We often dress in colors, patterns, and textures based on how we feel or want to feel on any given day. If you have an important business meeting or the interview of your life, you dress to the max. Your outfit might be black or red because you're in a power mode. When your lounge-lizard mode kicks in and you intend to vegetate in front of your television all day long, you slip into a pair of old, comfy sweats and a grungy T-shirt to reflect that mood. You've been invited to an outdoor party so you wear a colorful shirt or sundress drenched in yellow, blue, or green to represent your festive, energetic mood.

Question Three: Your Favorite Body of Water

Your favorite body of water represents *how you see sex for you.* Maybe your answer was Hot Tub: hot, steamy, and relaxing. For you, sex might be an extremely intense, relaxing, and passionate endeavor that you use to relieve tension. This comes from water as it relates to the womb, sensuality, and sexuality.

Question Number Four: Your Most Beautiful Scene

Your most beautiful scene represents *your life or an intense, romantic involvement.* The dramatic and permanent loss of that scene represents your death or how you would react to the sudden, unwanted, unexpected termination of a long-term relationship that wasn't caused by you. We hope you value your life and relationships and assume that the loss of either would cause normal feelings such as anger, denial, fear, depression, frustration, loneliness, devastation, and sadness. However, from those with a more grounded spiritual base who handle closure better, answers such as acceptance, gratefulness, serene, hopeful, and complete are common. This doesn't mean that you're ready to get dumped or for your own death. It means that if you were to die or get dumped, you'd have no regrets. You'd go out cleanly, with little to no baggage. You've cleaned your house emotionally, lovingly, and have lived fearlessly, allowing more complete closure.

What *In Through the Out Door* allows is a glimpse into people's subconscious, secret, or blind areas—ones they'd normally guard or be unconsciously aware of. Instead of getting conscious, padded, or pat answers, you'll get a more genuine feel for their positions on sensitive topics. You're covering touchy subjects without being intimidating or probing. Another reason we recommend this exercise is that it's fun and promotes some good-natured communication.

INCREASING YOUR DESIRABILITY AND EMOTIONAL STAMINA UNDERSTANDING PACE, PATIENCE, AND PASSION

It's not enough to "survive" the first few dates, especially if you're shopping for a mate. In the first 90 days, you'll set the stage for a longer-term relationship and discover the substance of your character (and theirs). When you find what you think could be a great relationship choice, it's easy to be overwhelmed with infatuation, anticipate more than is appropriate, and throw common sense to the wind. Human emotions tend to be like greyhounds at a dog race—always chasing the elusive rabbit, living off the "rush" and burning out when they fall short. Strong emotions can only sustain for a short distance; they can't handle the long haul. Like the hare who raced the tortoise, when we run our engine at full tilt, without saving energy to reach the finish, we burn out. By approaching a new love interest with a slower, steadier pace like that of the tortoise, you'll be more likely to "finish the race" and gain the long-term relationship success you desire.

While you're prepared to make a better pick right out of the gate, further investigation by means of time spent with the chosen person may reveal personality and character glitches. Some may warrant an immediate escape; others can be over-

> 66 Human emotions tend to be like greyhounds at a dog race—always chasing the elusive rabbit, living off the "rush" and burning out when they fall short. 99

come. By emphasizing patience, we hope to prevent you from prematurely ending a relationship that could have stood the test of time with long-term success.

PACE

The pace of the relationship will dictate how long it will last. Our goal is to transform you from a sprinter into a marathoner. Most people get so excited about their new romantic interest that suffocation is inevitable. Too much intensity by one or both parties is almost a guarantee that the relationship will self-destruct. Slow down! Love that lasts is more like a chess match than a video game. Chess is a well-thought-out, focused, strategic, studied, savored game in which quick, irrational moves can lead to disaster. A video game is often more flash than substance, intense but over in a few minutes (if you survive the initial stages), and reactive in nature.

> 66 Too much intensity by one or both parties is almost a guarantee that the relationship will self-destruct. 99

How fast is too fast or too much? Five phone calls per day, three e-mail messages by lunch time, and seeing each other six days a week is like jumping out of an airplane without wearing a parachute. What provides a huge initial rush will be over quickly, and the landing can kill the relationship. Leave some mystery! A phone call or e-mail once every few days is more interesting, gives you more to talk about, and creates anticipation as you hear the person's voice or see his or her name on your screen. How often you see each other depends on your ability to integrate into each other's lives and coordinate schedules without interfering with what you already have planned. Time spent together should be no more than you'd spend with a new friend and changes in your own lifestyle should be minor.

If you begin excusing yourself from commitments you had before the relationship, such as early work hours, sports or working out, or time with family, friends, church, or volunteer endeavors, then you're probably overinvesting too soon. It's different if your love interest is proportionally integrating into those activities, such as attending church with you, working out with you and your friends, or playing on your teams. Your friends, family, and other activities or obligations will still need some undivided attention.

Independence is the key to preventing relationship saturation. People with children must maintain their schedules and responsibilities when incorporating a new romantic interest into their lives. Remember, you're the one who's head over heels, not your children. Letting them get used to the new person's presence gradually shows respect for their feelings.

What's a reasonable pace within the first 90 days? Seeing them one day or evening during the week and four or five hours once or twice during the weekend is reasonable. Of course, holidays, birthdays, special events, or major activities might increase contact. If you're in the neighborhood at lunchtime, it's fine to share a meal. The slower you go, without stalling out, the more likely you are to create a greater level of desirability.

When should you introduce your new love interest to your close family and friends? Timing is everything. If you introduce them too quickly (less than 30 days), it puts tremendous pressure on them to "perform" and, if it doesn't work out, makes you look like a revolving door who can't keep a good catch. But if you wait too long to introduce them to close

family and friends (past 60 days), it sends a message that you may be embarrassed to show them off or are unsure the relationship will succeed.

Gift Buying

Gift buying and receiving also send strong messages. The buying and receiving of gifts should be appropriate and proportionate to how long you've been dating. Should you bring a gift on a first date? No. (The date *itself* is a gift!) It's appropriate to begin giving gifts when it fits the occasion, when it's from the heart or for the heart, and when it's a thank you or compliment with no ulterior motives or intentions implied.

When it comes to gift buying, we suggest the following guidelines:

◇ **Don't outspend the other.** Don't spend more than one and a half times what they probably spent on their last gift for you. If you know that their gift to you cost approximately $10, don't spend more than $15 on theirs.

◇ **Avoid gift certificates.** They're impersonal, seem like an afterthought, and make you look indecisive or lacking confidence in decisions.

◇ **When in doubt, go in the direction of romance.** A dozen roses might mean more than a new sweatshirt or cookbook.

◇ **Never give a gift that's breathing (or one that should be and isn't!).** Examples include a puppy, plant, or fish (alive), and a fur, ivory necklace, or floating fish (dead).

◇ **Never buy a gift that infers their doing something for you.** Haircutting shears and cookware indicate you'll be enjoying a home-cooked meal with shorter hair.

◇ **Don't spend more than you should.** It's not the size or cost of the gift that matters; it's the care and thought behind it. Examples of low or no-cost gifts are a note on their mirror, home-baked cookies, a card you made, a T-shirt, or our personal favorite—fresh Hawaiian flowers.

When giving or receiving gifts, it's important to remember to never keep score and to give and receive humbly, graciously, and without conditions. The greatest gift you can give someone is your time and attention.

PATIENCE

Our goal for discussing patience is to help you discern between a *resolvable fault* and a *fatal character flaw*. Resolvable faults might include her getting makeup on your new, clean white towels, or his dog's stinking and shedding, or the fact that he (or she) simply looks a bit heavier in their swimsuit than you expected. While you realize your love interest may not be a "10," an "8" is far cry from a "5."

Many of these issues can be worked out and resolved. How? "I would really appreciate your using the black towels instead of the white ones for taking off your makeup." "Your dog is very active. You may need to bathe her more often." "I'm trying to get into better shape. Would you like to work out with me? It always seems so much easier when I work out with a partner."

We often delay discussing problems in the first stages of a relationship because we're afraid to lose what we have, or we think the other person might get hurt or offended. After reaching a boiling point, we may drop what's bothering us onto our partner like a bomb, before they're even aware that a problem exists. By gently approaching issues and discussing them soon after they surface, you can prevent explosive confrontations and unnecessary breakups. You and your partner can then work through the issues together and maintain self-esteem, satisfaction with one another, and success in your relationship.

Fatal character flaws usually can't be worked out. For example: to her, social drinking means: "Please insert I-V here." Or she calls you eight times a day to find out where you are, whom you're with, and what you're doing. Or the last five movies he chose revolved around bloody gore and hard-core action (can you handle another one?). What you're recognizing are qualities that you might consider "fatal"—impossible to live with on a long-term basis. When does your patience wear thin? When does an issue or behavior become unacceptable? How long will you go without bringing up an important topic for discussion? If you're constantly crying over how you're being treated or misused; if friends and family are expressing deep concern; if you're suffering recurring negative consequences as a result of your involvement with that person, it's time to consider ending the relationship. While we said that certain "faults" can be tolerated or corrected, those that you simply can't abide should motivate you to bail in a hurry.

> 66 By gently approaching issues and discussing them soon after they surface, you can prevent explosive confrontations and unnecessary breakups. 99

Patience involves having open-minded discussions while learning the art of compromise. Discussion is not synonymous with "attacking" another person's character. It involves addressing what troubles you before it festers and threatens the relationship. If you apply patience and discussion in cases where a relationship isn't going well, you'll soon look back at the "nearly" fatal flaws that you corrected.

Recognizing that a fatal flaw exists and not leaving soon enough keeps you trapped. You may become numb to what's unhealthy and end up back where you began. If you've been drawn into accepting fatal

character flaws in your significant other and hang on to the relationship despite all the warning signs, *seek professional help*.

PASSION

Pookie, schnookums, baby doll, princess, darling, honey, angel, prince, my little love muffin, hunk baby, hottie.... Nauseated? Slobbering and drooling over each other like two mad dogs in heat will not make for a long-term relationship. How many times have you seen someone "fall in love" much too quickly? How many times has it been you? Love at first sight is simply a figure of speech. If anything, it's actually lust at first sight. In this section we'll address physical chemistry, sexual speed limits, and sexual sensibility.

Physical Chemistry

In chapter 5 we talked about chemistry and hormones. In the early phases of a relationship, the hormonal drive we feel is a combination of newness, novelty, excitement, infatuation, and good old-fashioned lust. Arousal is part of human nature. A man's primary stimulation is visual, while a woman's is auditory. Many men get carried away by a mini-skirt and some cleavage wrapped in a bikini. Women prefer hearing how great they smell, how bright they are, how wonderful they look, and how much they turn you on.

God's little joke—making a man's sexual prime from his teens to twenties and a woman's from her thirties to forties—creates huge discrepancies in what each party desires and is ready for. To overcome the differences, make pace and patience your allies. Either you can try to fight nature or learn to appreciate, understand, and empathize with the other person's position.

Sexual Speed Limits

If a relationship progresses to an intense physical level of intimacy too quickly and lacks a foundation of friendship, respect, trust, communication, and commitment, failure is likely. What's left? Many people see sex as the pinnacle and culmination of dating. Taking spiritual and religious convictions into account, sex before marriage isn't an option for some people and is considered a deal breaker in whatever relationship they're involved in. If they feel pressure from you to violate their convictions, they're more likely to let go of you than surrender their spiritual beliefs and self-respect. Others would never consider buying a car they haven't "test-driven." Would you break in a perfect new automobile by going as fast as you can for the first 500 miles and then slam it into reverse? If you have sex too soon, you'll get a similar result. You can tear at each other's hearts, destroy the basic mechanisms that made your relationship run smoothly, and are likely to irreversibly damage a worthwhile investment.

> 66 If a relationship progresses to an intense physical level of intimacy too quickly and lacks a foundation of friendship, respect, trust, communication, and commitment, failure is likely. 99

The opposite isn't good either. Fifteen miles per hour on an interstate will make you an unpopular road hog. You may be controlling the relationship by withholding physical intimacy and using sex as a means of hostage taking. What gets you to your destination safely and efficiently is observing the sexual speed limits. Here are the road signs that will lead you to lasting passion:

◇ **Never cross a boundary you haven't been invited over.** "I want you to kiss me" versus "I'm not quite ready for that." Don't become an octopus. If your partner's reception to the level of physical contact you initiate is not warm, that's a clear sign that he or she isn't ready to go that far.

◇ **The best way to find out the speed limit is to ask.** "May I hold your hand?" "May I kiss you good night?" A little respect goes a long way.

◇ **Honesty is the *only* policy.** If you know you have a STD such as herpes, venereal warts, AIDS, or other, you owe it to yourself and your potential partner to be open, honest, and up-front. Failure to do so not only puts the potential partner's health at risk, but opens you up for lawsuits, ridicule, and a harsh ending to that relationship or even your life if they are withholding similar information from you. Without trust, passion won't matter.

◇ **If you don't ask about their sexual health history, you won't know until it's too late.** Ask before you progress too far, not after.

◇ **Each person has acceptable sexual behavior and attitudes.** While skinny-dipping may be fun and spontaneous for you, the other person may be uncomfortable with such "playful" activity, even in private. Respect the differences.

◇ **You'll never again be with each other "for the first time."** Make it special, make it count, make it last. Don't go too fast. Meet their needs and exceed their expectations.

◇ **We rarely see couples experience long-term relationship success who have had sexual intercourse before "consistently dating" for at least 90 days.** Ninety days of consistent and focused dating allows for a foundation of friendship to evolve, romance to surface, consistent communication to develop, and fatal character flaws to appear (which provides an opportunity to bail before reaching a physically intense level). It also allows you to develop an awareness of each other's wants and needs, provides for interaction with their family and friends, and keeps you from succumbing to a hormonal rush. While we recommend at least a 90-day minimum, only you and your love interest can determine the pace that's most appropriate and comfortable for you. *It could be much longer, and in many cases will be.* If and when sex does occur, safe sex and birth control must be a non-negotiable two-way street.

Sexual Sensibility

We're concluding this chapter in the same manner that many of your dates will end—with a kiss. Sexual sensibility is much like the difference between the taste of a sour pickle and a chocolate sundae. Your date is almost over and it's *Showdown Time.* You're wondering whether to caress with your lips, lip-lock, suck face, swat spit, play tonsil hockey—in other words, kiss. Do we kiss? Don't we kiss? If I do kiss, will I seem too aggressive? If I don't, will I be considered overly conservative? Will it be wonderful or horrible?

Your fear of giving a kiss and worrying about how it will be received might be as intimidating as entering a shark tank wearing a side of beef. Will your kiss create ecstasy or cause nausea? Instant gratification or immediate repulsion? Keep in mind that the first kiss moment is probably as awkward for your potential partner as for you. Unfortunately, your uneasiness often translates into poor and rushed techniques, making the experience less than enjoyable. Depending on how many opportunities a person has had to experience physical intimacy, he or she may simply be naive, inept, or inexperienced about kissing.

Common kissing mistakes people make include having atrocious breath, leaping from kissing to other desires too rapidly, and teasing excessively. A bit of mystery can be arousing, but becomes frustrating

when taken to an extreme. People seldom risk asking their partners what they truly enjoy or what brings them the greatest pleasure. We rely on trial and error. As long as success outweighs error, this method can work. But you may be all charged up and ready for passion only to have your fire extinguished by an inept kisser. See the sidebar for descriptions of some of the worst kissers, as described by our clients.

To become an effective kisser, you need to anticipate as well as you participate; be as tender as you are aggressive and as able as you are willing; be creative and caring about the other person's pleasure as for your own. It also doesn't hurt to have great hands and a delicate touch. Depending on the situation, a light touch to the neck, cheek, or a firm yet sensitive hug can complement almost any kiss. The prelude to the kiss—eye contact, conversation, and setting—all lead to the right feelings and actions. But there's something to be said for practice, practice, and more practice. If you've dated nothing but bad kissers like the ones listed in the sidebar, consider a vow of chastity.

> 66 People seldom risk asking their partners what they truly enjoy or what brings them the greatest pleasure. 99

If you're lucky and smooching has left a succulent residue that has you desiring more, be careful not to mistake infatuation or lust for love. *Sexual sensibility is the ability to use pace and patience to temper your passion.* Kissing can arouse the senses enough for you or your love interest to lose your ability to think or behave rationally. Heavy necking on the first few dates doesn't necessarily mean your soul mate is wrapped in your arms. It's easy to think that this is "the one" during physical fun. Let passion evolve and the process of romance grow gradually to prevent "the love words" from being abused. Saying "I love you" too often

BAD KISSERS

◇ **Niagara Falls:** This sloppy kisser produces enough liquid for a regatta. Towel, anyone?

◇ **The Cadaver:** This sort totally lacks emotion and makes no effort to reciprocate a kiss. It's like kissing the deceased at a funeral. Check for a pulse.

◇ **The Octopus:** Once you begin kissing, you'd swear they've grown eight arms because you feel hands all over your body. (Some don't consider this a negative kissing category!)

◇ **The Brillo Pad:** They haven't bumped elbows with shaving cream or a razor for days.

◇ **The Pile Driver:** Their tongue behaves like a drill bit on an Texas oil rig. Tongue in . . . tongue out. Tongue in . . . tongue out.

◇ **The Brander:** They leave their mark somewhere on your body to identify their territory. You may have to wear a turtleneck in the summertime after you've encountered one of these distant cousins of Dracula.

◇ **Up in Smoke:** Kissing this type is like using your tongue to clean a dirty ashtray.

◇ **The Sphincter:** Their lips are pressed so tightly together that you couldn't open them with a jackhammer.

◇ **Twister:** They're moving their tongue around inside your mouth at the speed of sound. You want to reach in, grab their tongue, and say, "What are you thinking?"

◇ **The Puppy:** They're licking you all over your face as if you were the ice cream flavor of the day.

◇ **The Grand Canyon:** As you're kissing them, you realize you can't touch the bottom of their mouth. You can't reach the top. You can't locate the sides. Their mouth is so large, it should have its own zip code.

◇ **Connect the Dots:** They rapidly and sporadically kiss your entire facial area as if they are connecting numbered dots into a picture.

◇ **The Desert:** They are so dry in the mouth it is like eating sand.

◇ **The Hoover:** They attempt to suck out your air, fillings, tongue—everything within their "grasp".

◇ **A Deer in the Headlights:** As you passionately kiss, you sneak a peak only to find them staring right back at you!

◇ **The Raw Oyster:** They're pale, cold, clammy, and have a chronic runny nose that oozes into the kissing area.

makes it a meaningless drone rather than an indication of serious affection. Its value and importance are disrespected and lightly regarded.

You may have an inability to tell someone how you feel or be afraid to be the first to speak the love words. It can eventually cause your potential love to lose interest and faith in the relationship, leaving them feeling empty, unsatisfied, and unsubstantiated.

> 66 Sexual sensibility is the ability to use pace and patience to temper your passion. 99

You've picked well and are making it through the initial phases of a relationship (see more in chapter 8). You're beginning to get yourself in good social fitness and have hopefully made a transition from poor picking to healthy choosing and from revolving-door relationships to a healthier love interest with a viable future. But it's not enough to improve. You need to be able to sustain a healthy condition on a long-term basis. As your relationship progresses, your needs and those of your love interest change—as does the relationship itself, as well as its goals. You need to be able to assess, adapt, and address these needs over a longer period of time.

Chapter 8 will get you thinking about the long-term health of your relationship. While you've worked to resolve your deeper issues in chapters 1 through 4, we eliminated the quick fix in chapters 6 and 7, and chapters 8 and 9 are designed to provide you with the tools necessary for relationship longevity.

8

Moving from
Date to Mate

More than once, you have probably dreamed of a relationship with someone whom you have only dated a few times. While it is easy to fall into these fantasies, especially with someone who appears to be your dream come true, it is important to remain level-headed and first decide whether you're truly ready to add another person to your life. Although you know more about relationships, are you personally ready to enter into one? Are you set for the challenges and prepared to adapt to a condition of "two equals one"? It's vital to remember that you're not just adding another person to your life. He or she will be integrated into all aspects of it—intertwined with your family, your circle of friends, your employment situation, your "free" time, your play activities, your sex life, and your financial condition. Conversely, you'll become integrated into your partner's life. How will this affect each of you? Do you both have the versatility to adapt to so many major changes? Are you both at a point in time in your life where you're willing and able to do it?

If you decide that you're ready for a relationship and all that comes with it, you must begin to understand and take into account the **Life**

> **It's vital to remember that you're not just adding another person to your life. He or she will be integrated into all aspects of it—intertwined with your family, your circle of friends, your employment situation, your "free" time, your play activities, your sex life, your financial condition.**

Movement Pattern (LMP) for each of you. Whether single or married, all of us have an LMP—a process or routine we follow to carry out the various aspects and responsibilities of our daily lives. For most people, LMPs consist of three distinct, yet overlapping components:

◇ Job or career

◇ Private and personal home life

◇ Social life

LMPs for some individuals are relatively fixed, rigid, or inflexible. Look back to your school days and you're sure to find a good example of this. Even without assigned seating in your classes, you may have always chosen the same seat. If one day you found someone sitting in "your" seat, you may have felt violated ("How dare they!"). Nothing actually changed about the class, the classroom, or your access to the instructor or the chalkboard, but your pattern was disrupted. It can be frustrating to be slightly out of sync with what was "normal," predictable, and acceptable for you.

The efficient use of time is a top priority for many single adults. Since many aspects in life are beyond our control, our Life Movement Pattern is one that we can have our way. Why are we so inflexible about our LMPs? We've become creatures of habit and settle

into behavioral routines that offer us optimal comfort and stability. What we're doing and how we're doing it has importance to us. We worry when a pattern is disrupted (such as a diet or exercise regimen) that it will be difficult to get back on schedule.

Patterns that become disrupted, for whatever reason, can be a source of frustration, anger, conflict, or even excitement. Therefore, single adults must ask themselves whether they're ready for another person to interrupt their personal Life Movement Pattern. Before making a permanent relationship commitment, both parties should examine and discuss their daily life patterns, goals, and expectations—together. Why? Because LMPs can change dramatically when another person becomes permanently involved in their life. How much time together is available for the relationship to happen and flourish? Your ability to negotiate the mundane and divide up the details and responsibilities, and your willingness to compromise, will be vital to the success of your relationship.

The hurdle most people face is an inability or unwillingness to sacrifice or modify individual patterns to assimilate their life with another person's. We assume that since you're reading this book you'd like to be involved in a successful relationship at some point in your life. So you can accomplish this, we encourage you to examine your **Commitment Readiness** to determine whether you're prepared to enter into a relationship as an equal partner. Here are some basic questions to help you evaluate your readiness for commitment:

1. Can you place another person as a top priority in your life?

2. Are you looking to have more fun and be more spontaneous?

3. Are you prepared to divulge private aspects of your life with another person and find out and accept his or hers?

4. Are your goals and dreams similar?

5. Are your expectations reasonable?

6. Will your travel or work schedules cause difficulty?

7. Where do you both stand on the topic of children? None? Many? Somewhere in between?

8. Are you ready to spend more time and money on leisurely pursuits?

9. Are you ready for a dramatic increase in your number of acquaintances and social commitments?

10. Are you ready for your spending patterns to change in order to include another person?

11. How many "fixed" commitments do you have on a weekly basis? How much time do these commitments require?

There are tradeoffs involved in maintaining a relationship: You must decide whether you want to alter your lifestyle to accommodate another person. You may find yourself choosing between loneliness or laughter, quiet times or confusion, control or spontaneity, open or guarded communication, no accountability or having to report your whereabouts to someone else, your parents or in-laws, and so on. The social dynamics are interesting and exciting when you allow another person into your life.

Let's assume that you had positive answers to most of the questions up above. We offer you the following exercise to assist you with your LMP and also to help you predict a person's (and your own) behaviors, wants, and needs.

THE WILSON LEANING PROFILE

The Wilson Learning Profile, developed by the Wilson Learning Corporation, is a wonderful assessment tool for predicting behavior.

This simple exercise will help you determine a person's basic social style so that you can address certain needs, wants, and behavioral attitudes, and anticipate how your personalities will interact. Below is a diagram that serves as a guideline for how responsive or assertive a person is. We'll give you the overall picture first and then take you through the exercise, step by step.

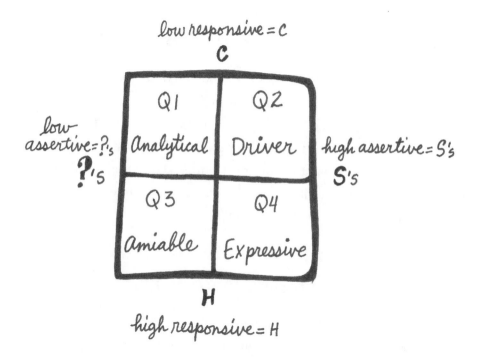

The four boxes comprise four quadrants that form a cross. Each quadrant represents a primary personality type. Descriptions of each type are below.

1. The upper left quadrant is the Analytical personality
   (Q1 = Analytical Personality)

2. The upper right quadrant is the Driver personality (Q2 = Driver Personality)

3. The lower left quadrant is the Amiable personality (Q3 = Amiable Personality)

4. The lower right quadrant is the Expressive personality (Q4 = Expressive Personality)

Q1: Analytical Personality

An analytical personality type is a low-responsive, low-assertive individual. The descriptions corresponding to this box show that people fitting this category tend to analyze much of what they do. They have a cooler, more analytical and calculated style. You may find them in fields such as science, accounting, or architecture. The specialty within this personality is technicality. These people are more reserved and pay great attention to detail. (C + ?'s = Q1)

Q2: Driver Personality

A driver personality type is a low-responsive, high-assertive individual. The descriptions corresponding to this box show that people fitting this category tend to control much of what they do. They have a cold, controlling, and aggressive style. You may find them in fields such as auto sales, real estate, or telemarketing. They're more confident, vigilant, and are somewhat exacting in their opinion. They believe their opinion is correct. The specialty within this personality is control. (C + S's = Q2)

Q3: Amiable Personality

An amiable personality type is a high-responsive, low-assertive individual. The descriptions corresponding to this box show that people fitting this category tend to be quiet, passive, and warm, yet unmotivated. They have a gentle, supportive, yet indecisive nature. You may find them in fields such as data entry, simplified factory assembly, or landscaping. They blend with others in their environment as they take on a passive role. More often than not, they're followers rather than leaders. The specialty within this personality is being supportive. ($?$'s + H = Q3)

Q4: Expressive Personality

An expressive personality type is a high-responsive, high-assertive individual. The descriptions corresponding to this box show that people fitting this category tend to be very animated, assertive, and outgoing. They have a warm and playful style. You may find them in fields such as bartending, acting, hair styling, or public speaking. The specialty within this personality is social presence. (H + S's = Q4)

(H can also stand for Hot, C can stand for Cold, S can stand for makes more Statements than asks questions, ?'s can stand for asks more Questions than makes statements. Each one of these is a point on a continuum. (A continuum is a line that is used like a scale to measure between two points.) For our purposes, if the middle of the line were "0" and the end of the line was equal to "+10" in any direction of equal segments, then we want you to mark anywhere but "0" on a scale of 1 to 10 in the appropriate quadrant the degree to which the description of that segment of the line or quadrant best matches your personality or that of the person you are attempting to analyze.

Here's a brief list describing each point on the continuum.

Low-Responsive [C] Characteristics:

People falling into this category are reserved and unresponsive—poker-faced. Their actions are cautious or careful. They want facts and details. Their eye contact is infrequent while listening and their eyes convey a harsh or serious emotion. They limit use of their hands, keeping them clinched tightly, folded, or pointed. They limit personal feelings, story telling, or small talk, and often appear preoccupied or vigilant.

High-Responsive [H] Characteristics:

People falling into this category are animated and use facial expressions. They smile, nod, and frown, and have a friendly gaze. Their actions are open or eager. They make little effort to push for facts and maintain frequent eye contact when listening. They keep their hands free and their palms up in open, friendly gestures. They share their personal feelings and are attentive, responsive, and enjoy relationships.

Low-Assertive [?'s] Characteristics:

People falling into this category seldom use their voice to emphasize their ideas. Their expressions and posture are quiet and submissive, and they tend to lean backwards. They're deliberate, studied, or slow in speech, and show indifference with their handshake. They ask questions more often than they make statements, and are often vague and unclear about what they want.

High-Assertive [S's] Characteristics:

People falling into this category emphasize ideas by a change in their tone. Their expressions are aggressive and dominant. They're

quick, clear, fast-paced, and have a firm handshake. They often make more statements than ask questions and are quick to let others know what they want. They tend to lean forward to make a point.

HOW TO USE THE
WILSON LEARNING PROFILE

Continuum A. If you're doing this exercise on yourself or with someone else, place an X on the line in the spot that's representative of where your (or their) personality would fall on the continuum. Your choices are a person who asks more questions or a person who makes more statements. If you ask a lot of questions and fit the low responsive descriptions we listed above, place an X on the far left of the continuum. If the opposite is the case, place an X to the far right. Don't place your X dead center because you would simultaneously fall into all four personality types, which is impossible. Picking just slightly left or right of center is fine.

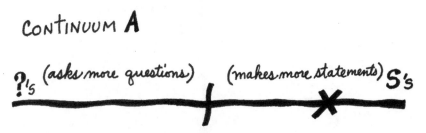

CONTINUUM **A**

?'s (asks more questions)   (makes more statements) S's

Continuum B. Place an X on the line somewhere representative of where your personality (or theirs) would fall on the continuum. Your choices are a person who has a colder or hotter personality. If you're a

cooler, more reserved, and less responsive individual, place an X near the top of the continuum. If the opposite is the case, place an X near the bottom. Again, don't place your X in the dead center because you would simultaneously fall into all four personality types, which is impossible. Picking just slightly above or below center is fine.

Continuum A & B. In the example on page 213, continuum A & B is marked and plotted. It shows that this person would be an expressive personality as he or she lines up in the quadrant for that description. Because the person was placed on the statement side of the continuum and the hot side of the vertical continuum, when you join the two points,

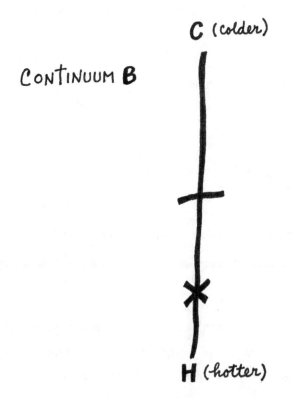

CONTINUUM A & B
(an example of an Expressive Personality)

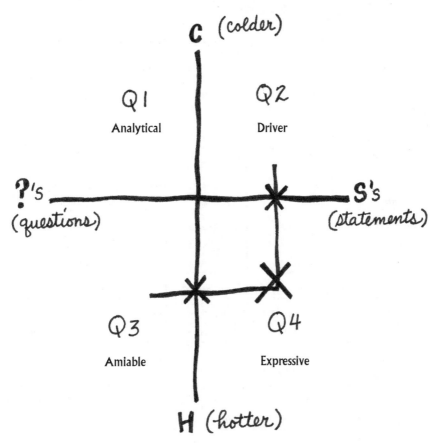

C (colder)

Q1
Analytical

Q2
Driver

?'s
(questions)

S's
(statements)

Q3
Amiable

Q4
Expressive

H (hotter)

it places them squarely in the expressive personality type. Thus, they will be outgoing, assertive, flamboyant, and a happy-go-lucky type of individual. Depending on where you plot yourself or others, simply refer to the descriptions of a Q1 through Q4 for an understanding of that personality type.

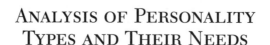

ANALYSIS OF PERSONALITY
TYPES AND THEIR NEEDS

Table 8.1   Social Style Summary

	Driver	**Expressive**	**Amiable**	**Analytical**
Backup Style	Autocratic	Attacker	Aquiescer	Avoider
Measures Personal Value By	Results	Applause	Attention	Activity
For Growth Needs To	Listen	Check	Initiate	Decide
Let Them Save	Time	Effort	Relationships	Face
Needs Climate That	Allows to build own structure	Inspires to their goals	Suggests	Provides details
Take Time To Be	Efficient	Stimulating	Agreeable	Accurate
Support Their	Conclusions & Actions	Dreams & Intuitions	Relationships & feelings	Principles & Thinking
Give Benefits That Answer	What	Who	Why	How
For Decisions Give Them	Options & Probabilities	Testimony & Incentives	Guarantees & Assurances	Evidence & Service
Specialty	Control	Social	Supportive	Technical
© 1975 Wilson Learning Corporation				

How can you use this chart in a way that can be beneficial to you?
Imagine that you are in a relationship with an *expressive* personality
type. This chart has everything you need to know about how to achieve
with the type of interactions you desire with this person. It will help you

predict her (or his) behavior, meet her needs, make decisions, reassure her, as well as address six other pertinent areas of your relationship. The personality type is listed across the top and the need or behavior is contained within the left column. The bottom row, her "Specialty" is simply a summary of her personality type.

Follow us down the column for the *expressive* personality as we relate these examples to you. Let's say that you're seeing an *expressive* personality type and are attempting to decide what to do on a date. Based on the chart, you would want to select an activity that is social in nature, stimulating to her, and allows her to save effort. Therefore, you might want to visit an amusement park rather than take part in an all-day, 20k walk. In choosing a restaurant, select a place that comes "highly" recommended by one of her friends so that she can check it out, enjoy it, and report back to her friend. When talking about your relationship, make sure she realizes how much she'll benefit from being involved with you and be sure to support her dreams and intuitions. Understanding the personality types and the Social Style Summary that best describes each will help you better understand people and thus stay a step ahead of the game.

When looking at your LMP, this exercise will make you aware that certain personality types will have very different LMPs. By utilizing the Social Summaries from The Wilson Learning Profile, you'll be able to meet, address, or compromise within your own LMP as well as satisfy your partner's to the best of your ability. Be aware that if two personalities are very far apart on the continuums, they will have very little chance of working together. The farther apart they are, the less flexible they'll be. The closer to center you are on either axis or the closer your potential partner is to your personality type, the more similar your LMPs will be. In this case, there will be less need for flexibility as your patterns will be closer to overlapping.

THE FIVE PHASES OF A RELATIONSHIP

A better understanding of the Five Phases of a Relationship will help you smoothly reach your relationship goal and have sweeter realities than dreams. Most relationships follow a very predictable pattern, as we will outline for you.

PHASE ONE: INFATUATION

During Phase One you meet or talk with someone and experience an "instant connection." It seems like you've known the person for much longer than you have. You can't stop thinking about him (or her) and begin to keep track of how often you do. Your appetite may diminish and time spent with him in any way seems to pass quickly and without effort. When it's over, you can't wait to see or talk with him again. When you're near him, you may feel a bit "tingly" and lack the ability to speak clearly and coherently. This is not a bad feeling—in fact, it's closer to wonderful. In your mind he appears perfect, absent of any faults, and can do no wrong. Your priorities and value system can get cast to the wind where he's concerned, and you're willing to take more risks or spend more money than you normally would. His happiness is your main priority.

PHASE TWO: DISCOVERY

Phase Two marks the end of being in "blind infatuation." You begin to realize that he (or she) is a human being with faults. You don't evaluate him or place a value judgment on his flaws; you just begin to notice that they exist. These are his perks and quirks, the queries and kinks that

are noticeable enough to raise an eyebrow. You can see all that glitters is not solid gold. While you're still very attracted to him, you realize that he has limitations and isn't perfect about everything as you once thought.

PHASE THREE: REALITY

Phase Three enables you to notice that certain faults, flaws, and personality characteristics may be permanent. Some of these appear on a consistent basis, while others are more shocking and short term in nature. You begin assessing their flaws in depth with a long-term relationship in mind. Real discussions begin as you become open to constructive criticism and feel comfortable criticizing the other person. During Phase Three, infatuation is replaced by true passion. Trust, respect, and intimacy become established as key elements in the relationship. By now, monogamy is expected, often a foregone conclusion. A serious deficiency in any one of the Five Characteristics of Healthy Love (found in chapter 1) is a clear warning that it might be time to call it quits and move on if an issue can't be quickly and consistently rectified. If either party has children, the success of adjustment is very important.

> 66 During Phase Three, infatuation is replaced by true passion. Trust, respect, and intimacy become established as key elements in the relationship. 99

PHASE FOUR: DECISION

You've reached the point where you can determine whether his (or her) flaws are terminal or acceptable to you. Should you continue dating

at the present pace and level of intention, continue to date with a more permanent outcome in mind, or call it quits? It's not just a matter of loving someone in healthy way. Is the feeling of being "in love" present and predominant? Do his assets far outweigh his liabilities? If liabilities exist, have you determined whether they're of a nature that you can easily live with?

At this point in a relationship, you should both be open to working together to modify what bothers each other to the best of your ability. How much money, time, emotion, and energy you've invested is no longer an overriding factor in whether or not to continue. Sincere concern, enjoyment, mutual respect, and admiration are the primary factors and focus. *Do you each enhance the other's life by being part of it?*

The decision to stay and move forward is the springboard to commitment. This begins the process of making your relationship more permanent. Barring trauma or a severe fault surfacing, you're well on your way to lasting longevity. The amount of time that passes between deciding to move forward and making a permanent commitment varies for every couple. Each person, in fact, must move at the pace that is most comfortable for him or her. But if you've asked all the right questions and spent enough time with your partner to assess their assets and their liabilities, and you're pleased with what you know and feel, you may be ready to make a more permanent decision.

PHASE FIVE: COMMITMENT

Will you . . . do you . . . could you ever see . . . is it possible . . . would you consider . . . are you busy . . . for the rest of your life? If you choose to proceed "full steam ahead," there are three possible outcomes for your relationship.

① **Your relationship will be enhanced.** This person is the love of your life and vice versa. You're in agreement about most things, share a certain passion and excitement, revel in discovery, and feel secure in your decision-making ability as a couple. As individuals, you shine a bit brighter with the light and encouragement the other brings to your life. You learn more about each other daily and like what you learn. You challenge each other in constructive ways and maintain your independence and identity while integrating into each other's lives. You know intuitively that you're right for each other and feel more complete as a result of being together.

② **Your relationship will maintain a stagnant course.** What started out as a refreshing dip now has you stranded in the middle of an ocean with no land in sight. You're not sinking; you're not swimming; you're simply hoping you'll get rescued. You or your partner may lack the skills to progress and grow or to keep your momentum moving forward. You may remain together out of a sense of obligation, which may be spurred by a tragic event such as an unwanted pregnancy, a devastating accident or illness (that left you or your partner in great need). Or, you may be afraid to end it because of all the time, energy, and effort you've invested to that point. We all desire a positive return on our investments. You may both simply be willing to settle for mediocrity—being together in any capacity beats being alone. Perhaps family pressures or your religious beliefs pushed you into a commitment that wasn't right or you weren't ready for. You may no longer feel a need to "impress" your partner since you're secure. Consequently, you let romance dissipate and disappear.

③ **Your relationship will regress.** Due to a lack of effort, loss of interest, a poor choice, or a tremendous fatal flaw (you caught her cheating,

for example), your relationship loses all cohesion and continuity. Issues beyond your control, such as lifestyle changes, age differences, or external disruptions (such as loss of job or extended family illness) can be factors that strongly contribute to the breakdown and instability of a relationship. Your ability as a couple or as individuals to seek outside assistance and support to overcome these external issues will be contingent upon your willingness to receive help. Failure to seek and find proper professional, qualified assistance before the relationship completely disintegrates will surely leave you with wounds that must be healed before you can successfully enter into a new relationship. If not, they'll come right along with you.

THE RELATIONSHIP BALANCE SCALE

In every relationship and each facet of that relationship, one person will put in more effort than the other. One or both partners may be incapable or unwilling to contribute fully or equally in a given area at a given time. The Relationship Balance Scale is an assessment tool used to determine:

◇ Whether your relationship is proceeding in a healthy direction.

◇ What degree of stability, health, and effort each of you brings to the relationship.

◇ How much effort each of you is putting into enhancing your own life and wellness.

Each person brings a measurable level of healthy effort to a relationship. The exercise below is designed to assess four things:

1. The perceived difference or similarity in effort levels, as you see it, between *you* and your partner on ten specific issues of *importance* to a relationship.

2. The perceived difference or similarity in effort levels, *as your partner sees it,* between him or her and you on ten specific issues of importance to a relationship.

3. Your overall compatibility score as you *both see it.*

4. Your personal score, which indicates how healthy you are as an individual, and what degree of effort and wellness you bring to that relationship.

Many exercises determine score values that rarely change over time and are relatively stable. This exercise can be taken weeks, months, or years apart and will give you an accurate gauge, at that time, of the health of your relationship and your individual effort levels. Be aware that during the early stages of a relationship, such as within the first six months to two years, it's common to score quite high on many items as the euphoria of newness is still evident. Time, complacency, routines, and taking each other for granted can diminish that score. If either of you see an area in need of work because of a diminished score, it's time to address that issue to keep your relationship moving forward, fresh, and functional.

How to Use the Exercise

On the left side are ten areas of vital importance to a relationship, an individual, or a couple's well-being. Across the top are two columns: one for you to rate yourself and one for you to rate your partner in each area. You should each complete the exercise independently. Don't compare scores until you've both rated each other in all ten areas and calculated your totals.

Each statement should be rated on a sliding scale from zero to ten. Choose a number between zero and ten that best defines your or their degree of effort in that particular area. If you feel that you or they are

void of any effort whatsoever in a given area, score it with zero (0). If you or they are showing maximum effort in a particular area, score it with ten (10).

EXERCISE

~

The Relationship Balance Exercise

Areas of Vital Importance	Your Score	Their Score
1. Maintaining physical health & exercise (including hygiene)	_____	_____
2. Sharing mutual responsibilities (including children)	_____	_____
3. Communicating with your partner (verbal, written, nonverbal, interest in the relationship)	_____	_____
4. Earnings and/or contributions to the relationship	_____	_____
5. Planning social time spent together	_____	_____
6. Developing friends outside the relationship	_____	_____
7. Spiritual beliefs and practice	_____	_____
8. Continuous self-improvement and initiative	_____	_____
9. Exhibiting affection, affirmation, and intimacy	_____	_____
10. Planning for the future	_____	_____
Totals:	_____	_____

How to Decipher and Compare Your Scores

Discuss each individual vital area together before jumping down to your total scores or overall differential as one or two areas may be causing a large overall difference. Here are examples of how two different couples might have completed the exercise, including their scores and what they mean.

EXERCISE (EXAMPLE)

Couple #1: Edna and Rupert

Areas of Vital Importance	Edna's Scoring		Rupert's Scoring	
	Edna	Rupert	Rupert	Edna
1. Maintaining physical health and exercise (including hygiene)	7	5	6	7
2. Sharing mutual responsibilities (including children)	9	4	5	6
3. Communicating with your partner (verbal, written, nonverbal, interest in the relationship)	8	3	7	4
4. Earnings and/or contributions to the relationship	5	7	9	3
5. Planning social time spent together	7	5	3	5
6. Developing friends outside the relationship	7	4	8	4

Areas of Vital Importance	Edna's Scoring		Rupert's Scoring	
	Edna	Rupert	Rupert	Edna
7. Spiritual beliefs and practice	8	3	3	8
8. Continuous self-improvement and initiative	5	1	4	5
9. Exhibiting affection, affirmation, and intimacy	6	3	8	2
10. Planning for the future	7	4	8	4
Totals:	69	39	61	48

EXERCISE (EXAMPLE)

Couple #2: Kim and Tom

Areas of Vital Importance	Kim's Scoring		Tom's Scoring	
	Kim	Tom	Tom	Kim
1. Maintaining physical health and exercise (including hygiene)	8	9	9	9
2. Sharing mutual responsibilities (including children)	9	8	8	9
3. Communicating with your partner (verbal, written, nonverbal, interest in the relationship)	8	8	8	8
4. Earnings and/or contributions to the relationship	9	9	9	9
5. Planning social time spent together	8	9	9	8

6. Developing friends outside the relationship	8	7	8	9
7. Spiritual beliefs and practice	7	5	5	7
8. Continuous self-improvement and initiative	8	9	8	9
9. Exhibiting affection, affirmation, and intimacy	8	10	8	10
10. Planning for the future	8	8	8	8
Totals:	**81**	**82**	**80**	**86**

HOW TO INTERPRET SCORES

In example one, you can see that Edna perceived a 30-point differential in her favor, while Rupert perceived a 13-point differential in his favor. There were also several vital areas where each perceived that they were putting in a great deal more effort than the other was. The disconcerting part of this equation is that they both perceived they were putting in the most effort. Therefore, the discrepancy in point totals is really 43 points. Is that a significant number? Yes. Is this relationship experiencing tremendous difficulty? Yes again. The fact that they've let themselves and the relationship degenerate so badly indicates that this relationship is probably heading for an end. If they don't work to correct their shortcomings, it's likely that their future relationships will yield similar poor results.

In example two, Kim and Tom displayed numbers indicating they're in a much healthier and happy relationship and they perceive they're equally and fully contributing to their relationship. As in any relationship, a few areas exhibited minor glitches. But none require immediate attention or threaten the relationship. Do Tom and Kim have a bright

future? Probably, as long as they both keep contributing equally and growing as people and as a couple within the relationship. Paying close attention to each vital area will increase their likelihood of long-term success as a couple and growth as individuals.

INDIVIDUAL SCORING BREAKDOWN

As you begin assessing your answers as a couple, it will be helpful to have a scoring system to follow as a guide to your discussion. Please keep in mind that these number breakdowns aren't absolute but should provide a relatively accurate portrayal of what's happening to each of you within your relationship. *If you or your partner scored:*

90 to 100: You're either an egomaniac, lost in blind love or infatuation, nearly perfect (or think you are), or newlyweds (congratulations!). It will be difficult for any person or relationship to maintain this level of effort or excellence for an extended period of time.

80 to 89: You or your partner is very healthy. You probably take good care of yourself and others, and have a strong desire to grow as an individual and a couple. Your relationship is probably in great shape.

70 to 79: You, your partner, or the relationship has some strengths and weaknesses. This is probably a longer-term relationship being evaluated and the novelty of a new relationship has worn off. You're still in relatively good shape, but any score of 6 or under should receive immediate attention.

60 to 69: You, your partner, or the relationship are fragile and lacking in several vital areas and will probably require professional help as individuals or as a couple to help get things back into shape.

50 to 59: You might have simply given up on yourself, your partner, or the relationship. You or your partner is numb from the amount of pain or frustration being experienced as an individual or as a couple. Whoever got this score should get immediate help, as the quality of this person's life and relationship are nearing an intolerable level, and he or she lacks even the basic skills necessary to things without help.

Under 50: You or your partner have profound problems in many vital areas and should probably seek professional help immediately or a good divorce lawyer. You either picked wrong or were the wrong pick. Counseling at this point would probably be for the purpose of closure only. But the individual's score indicates a strong need for him or her to work through many vital issues to improve, regardless of the outcome of the relationship.

YOUR PERCEPTION OF THE DIFFERENTIAL BETWEEN YOUR AND YOUR PARTNER'S SCORES

Please keep in mind that these number breakdowns again aren't absolute but should provide a relatively accurate portrayal of what's happening to you as a couple within your relationship. **If your scores reflected a difference between your totals of:**

0 to 10 points: Provided that both individual's scores are higher than 70, you're doing very well as a couple and any differences are sparse or limited to one or two vital areas. Any area where a difference of more than two points exists might need a minor adjustment and deserves discussion. Overall, you're a great match and probably contribute equally to the relationship.

11 to 15: You're a relatively good match and see most things eye to eye, but some imbalances exists in the level of effort in several vital areas. With discussion and mutual effort, the distance between these

differences can be substantially narrowed before they become a more serious problem.

16 to 20: Somebody is not happy and feels as if he or she is doing most of the work in the relationship. A serious problem or two exists within at least two or more vital areas, and failure to address these issues at this time could likely prove fatal to the relationship.

21 to 30: Many profound differences exist and if you're not receiving some type of professional help now, you probably should be. To account for this size of a differential, chances are one or both of you scored below 70 as an individual. Any chance of salvaging this relationship is contingent on both parties working diligently to resolve the key differences that exist, soon, and to improve as individuals.

31 and over: One of you or both are fed up and probably ready to terminate the relationship and move on. Insurmountable differences exist and may not be resolvable. At this level they're probably evident of permanent character flaws. To account for such a vast differential, it's likely that one or both parties scored below 60. If this is the case, a great deal of effort will be needed to correct the vital areas that you as individuals show the greatest weakness before this relationship or any other could have a chance for success.

CHECKS AND BALANCES

We want to remind you of something we said at the beginning of the book. When you take care of yourself, you're also taking care of your relationship. The Relationship Balance is designed to serve as a balance sheet between you and your partner to examine your health, their health, and the overall health of the relationship. To prevent itself from going belly-up, a business must take a regular inventory to know what its

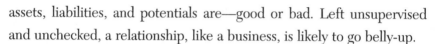

assets, liabilities, and potentials are—good or bad. Left unsupervised and unchecked, a relationship, like a business, is likely to go belly-up.

By looking at the examples we provided for Edna and Rupert, it's clear that from Edna's perspective this relationship is nearly over. Regardless of Edna's perspective, even Rupert recognizes that scoring as low as they did, both as individuals and as a couple, indicates a need for help immediately.

> 66 When you take care of yourself, you're also taking care of your relationship. 99

On the other hand, Tom and Kim have taken wonderful care of themselves. There-fore, they have the energy, passion, excitement, and resolve to put equally into a relationship. This creates two happy and healthy people who share a common life and mutual interests. How often you take this exercise is up to you. We recommend reviewing your relationship twice a year. Circumstances can change quickly and routines and bad habits can begin to set in.

HOW TO ANNOY THE OPPOSITE SEX

Why is it much harder to impress those who interest us than it is to annoy them? From loyal followers of our columns and seminars nationwide and those who visit our Web site (www.datingdoctor.com), we receive hundreds of letters weekly indicating how annoyed people are with the thoughts and actions of the other sex. Men frequently become annoyed with women and women with men. It seems that they often don't know how to communicate with or change one another and are simply sick of trying.

It's important to remember that people are human. When you spend considerable time with someone, specific things about that person will annoy you and vice versa—no matter how deeply you love one another. In the sidebars, we include the tongue-in-cheek lists both to entertain you and to demonstrate how *not* to treat a significant other. Do any of these behaviors sound familiar? (*Warning:* Taking these lists seriously could lead to undesirable results!)

It needs to be duly noted that the solution to good communication and a successful long-term relationship lies in your ability to *avoid* behaviors such as those described in the sidebars. Although our lists of techniques to annoy the opposite sex was tongue in cheek, you may notice some surfacing in your relationship. If this is the case, it's time to check the overall "balance" of your relationship and discover what's truly going on.

YOU'RE NEARLY THERE!

Experience has taught us that a little knowledge and insight will allow you to refocus your energies and choose paths that were previously unavailable to you. By now, you've probably noticed that you're attracting healthier people, are more attracted to healthy people, and are resistant to getting involved in the unhealthy types of relationships you had in the past. It's likely that as you've been reading this book and have begun to practice and use our techniques and develop your new skills, you've shared these new tools with others.

How do we best become proficient at something? We teach it to someone else. The more you practice what we've taught you—with friends, family, employers, colleagues, and your dates—the better you'll get at it and the more confident you'll become. Fresh insight is now your

WAYS FOR WOMEN TO ANNOY MEN

◊ Don't say what you mean—ever. Assume that he is clairvoyant.

◊ Be as ambiguous as possible. Master the phrase, "Oh, you know."

◊ Cry often. Tell him that it's his fault and that he should fully understand why you're crying because he caused it.

◊ Dredge up things he said or did weeks, months, or years ago and bring them back up during every subsequent disagreement.

◊ Constantly ask him loaded question such as: "Do you think I look fat in this outfit?" "What are your plans for tomorrow?" "Do you think she's pretty?" "Do you still love me?"

◊ Blame everything on PMS and his lack of feeling for what you're going through.

◊ Overanalyze everything he says or does, then analyze your analysis.

◊ Don't fake "it" but let him know that he's ineffective rather than a stud.

◊ Dress like a magazine model and then develop a 17-month-long headache.

◊ Ask him to do something for you and then complain about the way he's doing it

◊ Master the phrases, "You don't love me anymore. You don't treat me like you did when we first met."

WAYS FOR MEN TO ANNOY WOMEN

◇ Don't call her back—ever—after you told her you would.

◇ Skip the foreplay. Skip the chitchat. Act like it's a waste of time.

◇ Become an accomplished liar. Master the phrase, "Of course I love you, too."

◇ Talk about yourself often and remember, "The older you get, the better you are!"

◇ Scratch, spit, belch, fart, and adjust yourself in public. Be proud of your abilities and revel in your accomplishments.

◇ When on a date, never fail to point out all the other attractive women who are present and the exact reasons you find them so desirable.

◇ Forget anniversaries, birthdays, holidays, and other special occasions. Tell her that you're a man; therefore, it wasn't your fault that you forgot.

◇ When talking to other women in front of her, never look above their neck.

◇ When she asks you "loaded" questions, give honest answers. For example, if she asks, "Do I look fat in this outfit?" immediately answer with something like: "Huge would be a better description."

best ally. Your days of loneliness are numbered. Your social calendar is nearly filled. Friends and family have begun to notice a healthier, happier, and more productive individual in nearly every aspect of your life. Your future is as bright as your willingness to practice your new skills, resolve old issues, and initiate quality relationships with healthy and available people.

9

Your New Relationship Destiny

The information and techniques found within this book are designed to give you the skills and confidence to experience repeated success in your relationships. When was the last time your first date with someone led to a second, third, or fourth with that same person? Or do you feel as if you haven't been on a "real" date in ages?

When people reflect on what life has been like over time, many lament what went unaccomplished, or torture themselves trying to eliminate nasty habits that negatively affect their relationships. To inflict further self-abuse, they announce to all within earshot everything they've decided to change about themselves in the future while still lacking the tools to make that happen. Talk about setting yourself up for failure! If you know yourself better after reading this book and have realized positive changes through your own efforts or that of a good therapist or support group . . . BRAVO!

A CHANGE OF ATTITUDE

We challenge you to approach the process of dating differently. Begin to focus on your strengths, positive qualities, skills, and accomplishments.

Wouldn't it be nice to have no resolutions to make next New Year's Eve because you're living solidly in the solution, not wallowing in the problem? Instead of dredging up memories of every failed date or relationship from your past, chronicle your successes. What helped you meet the type of person you desired and become the type of person others desire? What did you do that was creative or innovative? What personalized your relationships? What did you use from this book that helped you become more successful? What do you need to practice more to build upon that success? Having done the work necessary to bring about change, what differences have others seen in you? What changes have you seen in yourself?

We need to reward our partners and ourselves when we excel as a couple or as individuals. We should acknowledge and accept others' good fortunes and share their wisdom. If friends or relatives are involved in a lasting and loving relationship, we should learn from them, rather than experience jealousy. It's no mistake when a couple is involved in a growing, satisfying relationship. They've taken the time and made the effort to reflect on what has been successful for them and capitalized on their strengths. They've avoided the dangerous propensity to look backward and say, "What if?" and have learned to look to the future and say, "Let's do it again, only this time, a little bit better."

You can't control another person's feelings or actions. You can only control your own behavior and hope it's appreciated. Although most people enjoy flowers, meals, movies, and presents, you can't buy a person's affection with gifts. A spark needs to be present and positive interpersonal chemistry must exist.

Instead of playing the dating game the way you think it is "supposed" to be played, take a more "game-free" approach and let your relationship evolve naturally. You're now equipped to know whether its evolution is healthy and whether you're with a truly caring, compassion-

ate, and loving person. You also can know whether you're such a person in return. Picking and dating still won't be "easy and effortless," but you'll be prepared to make better choices, for sounder reasons.

If you've been absent from the dating scene, pick yourself up, dust yourself off, review this book, and jump in with both feet. Keep your eyes and ears wide open. You might find yourself dancing through a wonderful evening on your way to romantic relationship. It all starts with asking. Whether you're a man or a woman, take a bold step and ask someone out or let the person know that you're interested and available. Passing an automotive dealership every day and eyeballing the car of your dreams won't get you closer to enjoying that new car. Sooner or later, you'll need to stop in and investigate whether it's worth owning, is compatible with your lifestyle, within your means, and will fully meet your needs.

The bottom line is that you are never going to date if you don't initiate. This can mean that either you do the asking or you make it clear that you are ready, willing, healthy, and available to date. It's not necessary to wear a sandwich board reading, "Date me now. Ask me how!" You can let others know of your interest and availability without going overboard or appearing needy. Make eye contact, smile, and return polite and warm gestures. Appear interested in people and what they have to say. Appear interesting yourself. Get out more and surround your-

> 66 The bottom line is that you are never going to date if you don't initiate. 99

self with available people. You need to expand your sphere of influence—people you meet through those you know or interact with. The more quality people you interact with, the better your chance of meeting someone who's available and right for you.

BARRIER BUSTERS

People often tell us how unsure they feel about how to begin and maintain a dialogue with someone they barely know, even if that person approached them and initiated the conversation. The "Barrier Busters" below are open-ended questions that enable people to gain confidence as they discuss familiar issues that interest them. Remember to tie in your *15-Minute Find* questions to keep the flow of conversation moving and to gain the information you'll need to decide whether or not the person is worth pursuing. Open-ended questions require more than a yes or no answer and lead to more interactive discussions. (*Note:* These Barrier Busters won't cover the first point of the 15-Minute Find Star, Physical Chemistry and Compatibility, because this area requires observation rather than verbal communication.)

Prime examples of Barrier Busters, the information each discloses, and the area of the 15-Minute Find each relates to include:

◆ What's the favorite place you've ever visited and why? (The extent to which they have traveled and what they value and why) (*PEG Influences*)

◆ Who makes you laugh more than anyone else in the world, and why? (What type of sense of humor they have) (*Lifestyle and Interests*)

◆ If you could trade places with anyone from history, who would it be and why? (Who and what impresses them) (*PEG Influences*)

◆ If you could be doing anything else with your life, what would it be and why? (Their goals, ambitions, and desires) (*Lifestyle and Interests*)

◆ What's your favorite movie? Television show? Actor? Actress? Type of movie? Why? (What entertains them and what they consider quality entertainment) (*Lifestyle and Interests*)

- Describe your best friend from childhood. What made you best friends? Are you still in contact with him or her? (Early childhood memories and feelings. What constitutes friendship) (*PEG Influences* and *Relationship and Closure History*)

- What have you recently witnessed that impressed you? (The skills they value in people and how easy or difficult they are to impress) (*Lifestyle and Interests*)

- What one thing have you accomplished that you are most proud of? (Feeling of self-worth and personal value) (*Lifestyle and Interests*)

- If you were casting a film about your life, who would play the main characters and why? (How they see themselves and believe others see them) (*Lifestyle and Interests, PEG Influences, Communication Skills*)

- What's your all-time favorite piece of clothing and why? (Most comfortable mode of dress) (*Lifestyle and Interests, PEG Influences, Communication Skills*)

- What stations are programmed into your car radio? (Musical tastes and style) (*Lifestyle and Interests*)

- What do you do to relieve pressure and stress? (Relaxation and "chill-out" preferences) (*Lifestyle and Interests, PEG Influences, Communication Skills*)

- What skill do you have that very few people know about? (Hidden talents and why they choose not to expose them) (*Lifestyle and Interests, Communication Skills, Relationship and Closure History*)

- Is there a difference between the "real you" and the "perceived you?" (How they see themselves, how they believe others see them) (*Lifestyle and Interests, Communication Skills, Relationship and Closure History*)

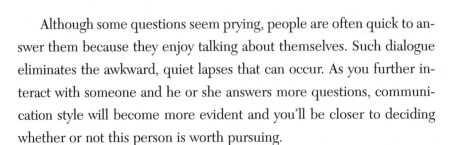

Although some questions seem prying, people are often quick to answer them because they enjoy talking about themselves. Such dialogue eliminates the awkward, quiet lapses that can occur. As you further interact with someone and he or she answers more questions, communication style will become more evident and you'll be closer to deciding whether or not this person is worth pursuing.

At the beginning of the book, we said that our job was not to fix you but to ruin your dysfunction. Don't be discouraged when life gets a bit uncomfortable or new situations feel alien to you. Practicing disruptive behaviors for years made you "comfortable" with the unhealthy. It will take time for your new attitudes and behaviors to become "comfortable" to you.

The perfect pick doesn't exist. No one can be flawless in every aspect of the S.T.A.R. (Someone Trustworthy, Available, and Real), nor should they be expected to be. Your goal isn't to put people under a microscope to find minute flaws as reason to avoid them. But becoming proficient at identifying features that may have attracted you to a poor pick, attracted a poor pick to you, or kept you involved in an unhealthy relationship in the past can result in a greatly improved partnership with a healthy individual in the future.

THE 15 BASIC PRINCIPLES OF RELATIONSHIPS

The 15 basic principles of a healthy relationship form the framework from which you'll build and maintain healthy, successful ones. They're what a skeleton is to a body or a frame is to a house. They're the foundation and basic tools to guide the decisions and changes you'll have to make in order to maintain in your new relationships. Several of these

were discussed earlier but we include them here to remind you what to do or not do for the best chance of finding and keeping a healthy partner.

1   **The people who love, care, or try the least have the most control.** They maintain this control because the other person in the relationship will do whatever it takes to change the attitude, demeanor, or behavior of a person who is less interested or invested. As much as we want them to, they'll never change their stance if they're getting everything they want out of the relationship without having to put much in. Let go of a lost cause. If you're consistently being treated poorly or putting in the yeoman's effort, move on. Your partner's lack of effort is sending a very strong message—stop and listen to it.

2   **Successful relationships don't begin by finding the right person.** They begin by *being* the right person. From the beginning of this book, you've gained tools to become the healthiest person you can possibly be so you can become relationship fit. As the book progressed, we taught you skills and strategies to use to discern a sound and healthy pick from a poor one—but look at which lesson came first!

3   **What was not resolved in past relationships will determine to whom you'll be attracted in the future.** You may have been involved with someone who rarely displayed physical love or affection, or someone who obsessed over you physically. You may have been in the habit of making your next pick the opposite of what you most recently experienced. But selecting someone at one extreme or the other is not the answer. In this case, the opposite of sick is sick; being healthy is somewhere in the middle. We're teaching you to date right, not to date a type. A happy medium will come from a well-informed decision, rather than a knee-jerk reaction to a previously uncomfortable circumstance or an emotional power surge.

4   **Opposites can attract, but we're actually drawn to the qualities and characteristics in others that we find lacking in ourselves.** If you're a quiet and reserved person, you may be attracted to someone who can walk into a room and immediately become the "life of the party." If you're gregarious, you may be attracted to someone who balances you by being a bit shy. As long as you're not looking to find and date your "therapist," and your qualities complement rather than annoy one another, this can be a workable and healthy choice for you.

5   **Anger results from the inability to achieve a desired outcome.** When two people are in conflict, it's easy for the disagreement to escalate to a point where one or both parties say or do something they'll regret. When involved in a disagreement, never attack the other person's character. When a judge informs a jury to "disregard the witness's last statement," you know they won't. The same applies to something said in the "heat of battle." You can apologize but never take it back. If you don't have to, don't fight. If necessary, fight a good fight, but fight fair. Stick to the facts, avoid accusatory statements, and listen fully to the other's side and opinions. Open-mindedness can and will open doors.

6   **People tend to repeatedly get into poor relationships because they seek out what's familiar to them and become good at what they practice.** We're essentially talking about brand loyalty. When you run out of a product you use on a daily basis, you usually go to a store and replace it with the same. Unfortunately, this holds true in relationships for people who haven't read this book! You date individuals who fall into a certain category and begin to repeatedly search for or attract this type. This cycle of dysfunction ceases when you learn what healthy is, become relationship fit, and deflect the people and issues that can interfere with relationships, happiness, and sense of satisfaction.

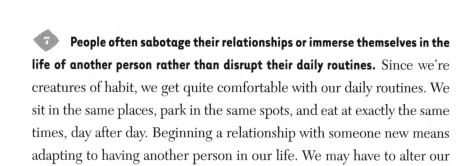

7 **People often sabotage their relationships or immerse themselves in the life of another person rather than disrupt their daily routines.** Since we're creatures of habit, we get quite comfortable with our daily routines. We sit in the same places, park in the same spots, and eat at exactly the same times, day after day. Beginning a relationship with someone new means adapting to having another person in our life. We may have to alter our daily regimen. For some people that's uncomfortable and unacceptable, so they sabotage the relationship by finding faults in their partner that may or may not exist, or concoct reasons why the relationship itself is wrong. At the other extreme, you may find someone who completely adopts your lifestyle rather than lose you or the sense of security a routine brings. This is as unhealthy as sabotage, possibly even worse, because they lose their independence and take yours as well.

8 **Forgiveness is choosing not to retaliate against someone who has wronged you.** Resentment can be defined as any emotion that controls you. The benefits of forgiveness are four-fold:

◊ You realize that you're mature enough to refrain from using revenge as a weapon.

◊ You realize that hurting someone gains you no advantage.

◊ You refuse to allow another person to rent space in your head free of charge.

◊ You owe them no amends as you didn't retaliate. At some point, they may even comprehend how wrong they were and make amends to you.

9 **Control issues are the most difficult topics for people to discuss sensibly.** These include issues relating to religion, alcohol, money, sex, power, politics, parenting, relatives, and relationships. People who thrive on feeling in control may even attempt to dictate the discussions that

revolve around control issues. Your ability to respect another person's opinion, whether you agree with it or not, is critical to developing trust, respect, and intimacy within a relationship. Couples who can't discuss issues sensibly avoid and push them aside until a time when they can no longer be suppressed. By then, the issues have often become sources of enormous friction.

10 Time makes people more human as their imperfections gradually rise to the surface. Your early feelings of infatuation will ultimately give way to clearer images of reality. If you can't get your love interest out of your mind or still believe he or she can do no wrong, give the person and the relationship some time. Just as you're not perfect, neither is he or she. You'll begin to discover what your love interest's imperfections are, face the reality of which ones are permanent, and have better information to base a decision about dating the person long term.

11 Loneliness and low self-esteem are powerful influences, leaving many people thinking that a poor relationship is better than none at all. Three Dog Night said it best when they sang, "One is the loneliest number." It can be so lonely, in fact, that many people will subject themselves to a far-less-than-ideal partner or circumstance just to avoid being by themselves. If you've been your own worst enemy, it's no wonder you've avoided a relationship with yourself. Until you become comfortable with yourself, how can you expect your partner or date to be comfortable with you?

12 Many women are attracted to "dangerous, emotionally unavailable" men, and many nice guys finish last. Women are attracted to "bad boys" because they're unpredictable, present a challenge to be won over, and appear in the minds of women "to be worth having." They rarely place

women number one on their priority list, which makes women desire even more to be the one to "break the wild horse." They truly believe they have what it takes to "change" him or "win him over," and that they're different from others who've tried. Emotionally unavailable men place little pressure on women as they give the impression that they can live "with or without them." You can equate the expression "bad boys" to "bad picks." They have earned their reputation.

Nice guys tend to lose out because they appear overly needy, divulge too much information too quickly, and try too hard to please and impress women. When men try too hard, too fast, it makes women wonder, "What's wrong with him?" What men like this fail to realize is that if a woman knows she can always *have* him, she'll never *want* him. "Nice guys" tend to be boring, present no challenge, are too predictable in their thoughts and actions, and are indecisive in their dating practices. They also give women this message: "You can date all the losers and bad boys you want. I'll be waiting when you come to your senses." There's one born every minute. (This scenario is not limited to women attracted to bad boys; many men are attracted to bad girls.)

13 **People don't grieve or review their failed relationships.** They simply replace them, having been taught over time that "there are plenty of other fish in the sea." How many people do you know who got rid of one spouse and replaced him or her with a clone? As a society we've been programmed to avoid pain at all cost and act like we haven't been adversely affected by loss. We've been taught to quickly turn to something else to suppress pain without evaluating what caused it in the first place. We're doomed to repeat mistakes and poor choices or get used to living with duplicates unless we change our patterns.

14 **You'll rarely, if ever, attract anyone healthier than you are.** If you do, it won't be for long. If you're not healthy, it won't remain a secret. As soon as a person perceives they are becoming your surrogate mother, father, brother, sister, or therapist, they'll bolt—for good reason.

15 **In order to have a lasting, loving and successful relationship, you must practice Trust, Respect, Intimacy, Passion, and Commitment.** Think of these five characteristics of a healthy relationship as the supporting legs on a round table spaced an equal distance from one another. When in place, the table is structurally sound. If you lose, destroy, or lack even one of these five characteristics in any relationship, it will weaken it—just as the loss of a leg weakens the stability of a table. The loss of two legs would make a table wobble and eventually fall, just as the loss of two or more essential elements would ultimately cause a relationship to collapse. Just as a table with only two legs is immediately useless, a relationship with only two of the five essential elements indicates an urgent and immediate need to end it. If these characteristics are missing, you're either involved in an unhealthy relationship, with someone unhealthy (or less than healthy yourself), or have experienced a traumatic event that damaged your relationship in ways that can't be repaired.

Let's assume that as a result of changes you've made, you are currently involved with a healthy pick. If that should lead to a long-term commitment, we have developed Ten Key Points to help you maintain an exceptional relationship (see sidebar).

 # KEEPING ROMANCE ALIVE

Just as the draft process is used in professional sports to improve teams through better draft choices, you may end up with a championship partner as your picks improve during your rebuilding process. But if you want to keep your partner around, happy and satisfied, and

keep the relationship moving forward and vital, romance must be nurtured and given a prominent role.

Here are several ways for men and women to be more thoughtful, spontaneous, and romantic to the other:

SUGGESTIONS FOR WOMEN: HOW TO PRACTICE ROMANCE ON MEN

◇ **Try not to be sports "clueless."** If his primary interests revolve around sports, and yours don't, try your best to become at least somewhat knowledgeable about his favorite ones and why they mean so much to him. Many women have become extremely athletic and knowledgeable about sports, which is either appreciated or causes apprehension in men.

◇ **Ask him out.** Offer to drive. Make the arrangements. Pay for the date. All he has to do is show up. This will be a huge change of pace for many men, and a wonderful and unexpected surprise.

◇ **Let him know that you appreciate his efforts and attention.** You need not constantly feed his ego or cater to him, but a quick and simple thank you from time to time can go a long way.

◇ **Drop him a note.** Send him a flower or prepare his favorite food. Everybody likes to feel special. It's a fallacy that men don't like receiving intimate gestures of affection such as flowers, romantic messages, or gifts from women. Most absolutely appreciate them though they're sometimes more reserved in showing their appreciation. You can be sure they'll gloat to their closest male friends about how awesome you are and how well they're being treated.

◇ **Be prompt in responding to an offer for a date.** Men appreciate decisiveness as it shores up their sense of security and self-confidence when they know they're one of your priorities. If you hesitate in

TEN KEY POINTS TO MAINTAIN AN EXCEPTIONAL RELATIONSHIP

To be involved in a healthy, balanced, and loving relationship, you and your partner must promise that you will:

1. Be honest, even when what you have to say may be painful to disclose. This doesn't give you the right to boss, control, or manipulate your partner. There's a fine line between constructive criticism and destructive hostility.

2. Practice romance that fosters passion. Perform unsolicited, ordinary gestures of love and affection at unexpected and expected times because you want to, not because you think you have to. Lose the scorecard! Your motives should be pure and "just because."

3. Discuss issues of importance rather than ignoring or suppressing them and allowing them to fester. Trust starts with the ability to practice intimacy. That includes your willingness to bring up difficult issues and follow them through to their logical conclusion. Work at learning the art of compromise, patience and understanding.

4. Manage your emotions, especially anger. Never go to bed upset, drive when angry, or resort to emotional or physical violence—no matter how heated an argument over an issue may become.

5. Maintain a sense of independence and a life of your own. Remember that your partner fell in love with you as an individual before you ever became a couple. That same independence and individuality can keep your relationship fresh, vital, forward moving, and alive.

6. Accept equal responsibility for and ownership of the relationship. Respect your partner's boundaries, goals, dreams, desires, and problems, and work together to help each other achieve or resolve them.

7. Make your individual condition a reflection of the health of the relationship. A balanced relationship begins with each individual being healthy in all major areas of his or her life. Maintain the best level you possibly can when it comes to physical, emotional, and spiritual health. Put this same type of effort into the health of the relationship and your partner.

8. Avoid taking each other for granted. Create new experiences together that will keep routines or systems from settling in and "stealing" passion from your relationship. Do not mistake serenity for boredom.

9. Support and allow your partner to maintain, practice, and grow within his or her spiritual belief system. In the event that your belief systems are different, support and respect your partner's values without trying to change them, and expect the same from your partner.

10. Commit to the excellence of the relationship. Use the skills and tools necessary to keep it healthy daily. Negotiate the mundane, celebrate the exceptional, hold each other in a positive light, and commiserate when necessary. Speak words of love. Stay active inside and outside the relationship with family and friends, and include each other in that activity. By committing to the health of the relationship, you're reaffirming your long-term commitment to each other and to the excellence that will accompany that effort.

responding to their offer, they'll believe your hesitation relates to them.

◇ **Don't check out or compare him to other men while you're out with him, as men are highly jealous creatures.** No further explanation needed.

◇ **Don't overreact when he wants to go out with the guys.** Encourage him to do so from time to time. This will provide needed breaks and time for you to spend by yourself or with your friends. Also, hanging out with the guys will make him appreciate you. He just might hear about how unhappy they are in their relationships.

SUGGESTIONS FOR MEN: HOW TO PRACTICE ROMANCE ON WOMEN

◇ **Pay for the date with class.** Don't make it a major production. There's nothing worse for a woman than to be made to feel as if she is obligated to you because you picked up a tab. It makes you look cheap and she may just develop a chronic headache.

◇ **Drop her an unexpected note, e-mail, or a poem.** You don't have to be long-winded—just sincere. Women appreciate knowing that you're thinking about them even when they are not around.

◇ **Actively listen and act on what she tells you.** If she mentioned in passing that she liked a particular restaurant, take her there. If you noticed her buying a particular magazine at a newsstand, get her a subscription to it. If you know her favorite color is yellow, bring her yellow roses. Showing her that you're alert, attentive, and thoughtful will be very impressive.

◇ **Don't pay attention to other women when you are out with her.** Never compare her or her attributes to another woman, especially when you're with her. If you're dumb enough to do it anyway, don't tell

her about it. Make her feel as if she's the sole object of your affection, which she should be, and not involved in a competition.

⬦ **Spend time alone with her.** Focus on her. Take her away from her everyday routine and lifestyle. It doesn't have to be expensive, just a diversion. Take her on an unexpected weekend getaway or suggest that the two of you visit her parents. Take her shopping and actually be involved, appear interested, and don't complain. Go grocery shopping with her for all her favorite foods then prepare a candlelight dinner that you make from scratch. Make sure you clean up your mess as well! Her only effort should be to enjoy the meal.

⬦ **Avoid checking your watch as if the time you have available to spend with her is limited.** Women appreciate knowing that they're a welcome part of your life and you enjoy their presence. They should never be made to feel that you're altering your day or life to "fit them in" or that an hourglass is measuring the time you have to spend with them.

⬦ **Practice chivalry with no ulterior motives in mind.** Open doors for her when you get there first, but don't race ahead and make a scene. Offer her your coat if and when she might be cold. Leave a brief message on her voice mail when you know she's not home. Drop her an e-mail to say you were thinking of her. Bring her a flower simply because it's Wednesday. The unprompted, unexpected, and romantic gestures of love mean the most.

As a result of being in an exceptional relationship, great things will happen. If you're both contributing equally and fully to an exciting partnership, you'll reap the tremendous benefits from that investment. As you practice romance on one another and develop a deeper level of commitment and satisfaction, certain promises will be realized. Some may come true more quickly while others may take a bit more time, but they will always be realized if you work diligently for them.

THE TEN PROMISES OF AN EXCEPTIONAL RELATIONSHIP

What you put into a relationship is what you'll get out of it. The first-class effort you put in will yield fantastic rewards. Here are the ten promises of an exceptional relationship and the primary focus of each promise:

1 You'll comprehend love, feel it, and practice it with each other as well as with others. (Complete and Unconditional Love)

2 Feelings of loneliness, frustration, and relationship despair will be over, and your social calendar will be filled. Hopelessness will be replaced by self-confidence. (Fearlessness)

3 You'll experience a sense of security, serenity, and peace of mind. (Stability)

4 Your past will no longer "haunt" you, as you are now involved in a new partnership for your future. (Resolved Relationship History)

5 Selfishness, self-centeredness, and a defensive approach will no longer be necessary. You'll experience joy, a sense of trust, and mutual interests. Thinking of yourself first will become secondary. (Healthy Sacrifice and Compromise)

6 Your success and ability to model it for others will create in you an exceptional attitude, as well as a sense of belonging, accomplishment, and change. (Quality Presence)

7 You'll never again face problems or pitfalls alone. (Mutual Security)

8 You'll experience and revel in lasting emotional and physical passion. (Fulfilled, Desired)

9 You'll become a stronger, happier, more complete individual and no longer accept unhealthy, disruptive, or destructive behaviors or attitudes. (Healthy Independent Identity)

10 You'll be comfortable with the success of your relationship and no longer feel a need to sabotage it or self-destruct. (Worthiness and Commitment)

 # OUR GIFT TO YOU

Although it may seem as if you've developed X-ray vision, for the first time you're viewing yourself, other people, and relationships as you should. You're noticing what's on the inside as well as the outside, and are alert to your needs and the potential of others to fulfill them.

The key is to exercise patience and realize that you may experience a few "speed bumps" along the way. Yes, you've gained the tools and confidence necessary to become the person you've always wanted to be and attract the partner you've always desired. However, you'll not become a "master craftsman" overnight. It takes time and practice before the many techniques we shared become second nature to you so you can transform your dreams into lasting realities.

Think back to where you began and look at where you are now. You now know what makes a good pick and understand what factors have

kept you from making wise choices in the past. You know how to find someone trustworthy, available, and real, as well as the process that needs to be followed to give your dates a great chance for success. You can identify the components of a healthy relationship, and discern when one is completely out of balance. You can spot the red flags, which warn that a potential pick wouldn't be good for you. If a relationship doesn't seem to be working out as planned, you have a basic knowledge of why, when, and how to call it quits. You've been introduced to exciting new definitions of age-old terms, which may have been less than healthy in the past but now have functional meaning for you. You have a foundation to rely on and a direction to follow that will enable you to attain, maintain, and surpass all expectations for a healthy partner and successful relationship.

The most important aspect of the book goes well beyond the changes it can create in your dating life and lifestyle practices. It even goes beyond the future that you can build by incorporating its principles into your life. Whether your goal is to find, date, or even mate with a healthy partner, we want you to have fun by *dating smart.*

There's nothing in this book that you can "do wrong." There are no right or wrong answers to any of the exercises, assessments, or tests you took. View them as a way to find out where you're coming from, where you're headed, and where you need to improve. Don't take them, yourself, or life too seriously. Work hard and be satisfied with doing your best to become the person your creator intended you to be—happy, joyous, and free. Above all, have as much fun as you can possibly stand, and may you soon have somebody special with whom to enjoy all the fun!

"May you have sweet dreams and even sweeter realities."

Thank you for sharing the time of your life with us.

Rick and Dave

INDEX

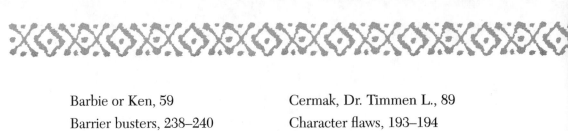

G

H

I

Mental illness, 159

Military Max, 166

Minimum dating standards, 27

Mis-prioritizing, 84

Mismanagement, crisis, 83

Mistrust, 80

Morals, 161–162

Moses, 23

Mothers. *see* Parents

Motivation, 27–28, 112

Movies, 154–155

Mr. nice guy/Ms. great gal, 57

Mr./Mrs. freeze, 55

Ms./Mr. perfect, 59

Mugger, 55

Music, 154–155

Mutual resolution, 167

N

Name, remembering, 179

Narcissus, 56

Nature of shame and abuse, 17

Needs

    control, 236

    desires *vs.*, 112–113

    familiarity, 242

Niagara falls, 200

O

Obessive-complusive disorder, 104–105

Octopus, 200

Of Human Window, 180

Office romances, 108

Oil and water, 166

One hundred yard dash, 54

Overanalyzing, 182

P

Pace, 190–193

Panhandler, 53

ParaSnooper, 103

Parental picking exercise, 29–36

Parents

    divorce, 126

    emotional pumps, 115–117, 120

    partner selection, 29–36

    status, 158

Passion, 195–202, 248

Patience, 193–195, 253

Pavlov's dog, 166

Perception

    others, 186–187

    self, 187

    sex, 188

Person, right, 241

Personal enjoyment, 26

Personalities

    amiable, 209

    analytical, 208

    changing, 236

FOR MORE INFORMATION

The authors offer seminars for a variety of audiences nationwide throughout the year.

Collegiate, Church Related, Singles, and Organizational Seminars:

Creative Dating: The Cure for the Common Relationship

Date Smart! Is it Love at First Sight or Done at First Sight?

Becoming a Legendary Man

Becoming An Exceptional Woman

Fanning the Values Flame

Two Hours to a Team

Who . . . Yeah! Building Communities out of Classmates

20 Key Points Every Freshman Should Know

May They Follow Your Path, Not Your Footsteps

(Parent's Orientation Program)

Let's Cut the Crap: How to Get Things Done (For Real!)

As an Organization

Leadership As a Lifestyle

Many of the seminars listed above are also available for corporations.

Corporate and Professional Seminars:

Emotional Productivity: Improve Your Employees' Lives and You'll Improve Their Performance!

For more information (including availability and price) or to schedule a seminar for your school, organization, or business please contact:

Diane Coleman
Agent and Account Manager
Coleman Productions, Inc.
and One Love, Inc.
P.O. Box 235
Loveland, OH 45140
(513) 583-8000 (Phone and Fax)
www.datingdoctor.com

ABOUT THE AUTHORS

David Coleman knows first-hand about healthy relationships. He enjoyed a happy childhood in a loving home where his parents survived to celebrate their 50th wedding anniversary and his much older sisters spoiled their younger brother. He went on to receive both his Bachelor of Science Degree in Speech Pathology and Audiology and his Master of Arts Degree in College Student Personnel Administration from Bowling Green State University. It was at his job as Student Activities Director at a private college in Cincinnati where Dave first designed his Creative Dating program as part of student orientation. By chance, a few weeks later, a presenter at a major Washington, D.C., conference cancelled and Dave stepped in. The response to his session was enormous, with *The Washington Post* and *Glamour* magazine running favorable stories and hundreds of radio and television interview calls pouring in. Fifteen years later, Creative Dating is a nationally acclaimed program, observed by over 1,000,000 people at college campuses, singles' organizations, churches, and other groups across the country. It has won the National Lecture Program of the Year by Campus Activities Today Magazine and the National Association for Campus Activities (NACA) on four separate occasions. Dave was named national lecturer of the year by *Campus Activities Magazine* for the year 2000.

Dave now devotes much of his time to running Coleman Productions, Inc., which represents Creative Dating as well as several of the top speakers and performers in the nation. He lives in Loveland (yes, Loveland), Ohio, with his wife, Diane, of 14 years, his two daughters, Shannon and Natalie, and his collies, Louis and Misty.

Richard Doyle has led quite a different life from that of his co-author. Born to alcoholic parents who were each married once before, Rick began using drugs and alcohol at the early age of nine and 1/2. His addiction continued until he was 20, when he went into treatment in January of 1981. In his first year of sobriety, Rick spoke at many schools about his usage and recovery. One woman in particular noticed Rick's speaking talents and offered him a job as a consultant with the Department of Human Services designing sobriety classes and lecturing on drug and alcohol addiction to foster care parents, adoptive parents, and case workers. Rick went on to become licensed as a Certified Chemical Dependency Counselor and Addictions Therapist at the highest state and national levels and was qualified as an expert witness in addictions and its related issues for numerous courts. He has served over 25,000 clients in two states, testified in hundreds of custody cases for the Department of Human Services, and worked as a senior therapist and legal liaison at a methadone clinic. After private practice for ten years, specializing in women's recovery/abuse/trauma and relationship addiction, Rick gained unique insight into revolving-door relationships. His personal recovery of 19 years and his 17 years as an addiction therapist allows him a perspective that says, *I understand*. His experience has made him a frequent guest on television shows and led him to write for numerous newspapers and magazines.

Rick is a lecturer for Coleman Productions, Inc. as well as One Love, Inc., a company which he serves as president, committed to providing resources, programs, including the *Date Smart* lecture program, products, and services to enhance and improve relationships. Rick lives in Cincinnati, Ohio, and spends much of his time writing, lecturing, and nurturing his Harley Davidson passion.